Gladys Henderson
5922 Johnnycake Rd.
Baltimore, 7, Md.

Understanding
The Methodist Church

NOLAN B. HARMON

BOOK EDITOR OF THE METHODIST CHURCH

Understanding The Methodist Church

THE METHODIST PUBLISHING HOUSE

Nashville	*Cincinnati*	*Chicago*	*New York*
Dallas	*Richmond*	*Baltimore*	*Kansas City*
Detroit	*Pittsburgh*	*Portland*	*San Francisco*

UNDERSTANDING THE METHODIST CHURCH

Copyright MCMLV by Pierce & Washabaugh

Library of Congress Catalog Card Number: 55-5738

B

SET UP, PRINTED, AND BOUND BY THE
PARTHENON PRESS, AT NASHVILLE,
TENNESSEE, UNITED STATES OF AMERICA

Foreword

To UNDERSTAND The Methodist Church, one should know something about its:

> HISTORY, and how it started
> DOCTRINE, or what it believes
> DISCIPLINE, or rules for conduct
> ORGANIZATION, or how it works
> WORSHIP and SACRAMENTS
> ACTIVITIES and WORLD-WIDE PROGRAM
> RELATION TO OTHER CHURCHES

In addition a modern Methodist Christian will want to know how he best can fit into his church's life and in the hurried rush of present-day existence make his time count more definitely for God and his Church. Written primarily for laymen, this book will endeavor to explain Methodism from the point of view of the local church.

A popular book of some years ago, *The Methodist Armor,* by H. T. Hudson, suggested the general plan of this volume; and many sentences and quotations from *The Methodist Armor* have been reproduced in these pages.

My interpretation of the Articles of Religion, the General Rules, and so must stand on its own merit, though my treatment of these has been checked by eminent authorities on Methodist theology and life. Many helpful suggestions have been contributed by these authorities and embodied in this book.

Understanding The Methodist Church does not attempt to cover all important matters of Methodist life and law which are set forth in the book of *Discipline* of The Methodist Church. That book—the official book of doctrine, discipline, and law of the Church—should be in the homes of our people and may be referred to for many matters which necessarily could not be treated in this brief volume. Here the attempt has been made to interpret the *Discipline* in its most important provisions as well as to explain to present-day Methodists many things which have to do with the practical working and high goal of their beloved Church.

Understanding The Methodist Church is published with the hope that it may prove inspirational as well as informative, and that because of it people will want to become better Methodists—which means better Christians.

NOLAN B. HARMON

Contents

CHAPTER ONE

How It Started

METHODISM began in the year 1729. It began in Oxford University, England. While at college there John Wesley, Charles Wesley, George Whitefield, and a few other young men banded themselves together for the purpose of intellectual and spiritual improvement, and to help one another become better Christians. So systematic were these young men in their habits of religious duty and so regular in their rules of conduct that gayer students in derision called them

METHODISTS

and the name stuck.

In like manner disciples of Christ were first called "Christians" at Antioch by a deriding world, yet the name was appropriate, and Christians have always gloried in it. Methodism, too, has had from the first a glorious history, and none of its followers is ashamed of the name. John Wesley himself often referred to the "people called Methodists."

The Methodist movement started not with the idea of founding a church or of reforming the world, but in the earnest desire of a few young men to live better lives themselves. That was all there was to it. These young collegemates at Oxford came together to encourage one another, to pray with one another, to study God's Word with one another.

They had no idea that they were starting the vast Methodist Church of the present—they simply longed for a closer walk with God and knew that they could help and be helped by one another if they met regularly and asked God to bless them. There were a good many other small religious societies over England at that time, and the "Holy Club"—another derisive name for the group—was not extraordinary except in the youth of its members and the fact that they were students in a cold, classic university.

The First Regular Methodist Society

The first Methodist society was organized in London in 1739 by John Wesley with about ten other persons. It soon swelled to hundreds, with other societies organizing in London and the English realm. A great revival of religion began to spread over the land and in time extended throughout the world. It was a work of depth and duration, and God was in it. Today, long after those beginning days, it still goes on and will go on wherever sincere souls, by whatever name they are called, continue to seek and find the way and will of God for themselves.

The Methodist movement came, as one writer said,

sweeping along like the winds which God had let loose from his fists, swaying devout souls, breaking down stubborn sinners, overturning hopes built on false foundations, but quenching not the smoking flax, nor breaking the bruised reed. It was Heaven's bountiful gift to the silent prayer of the world's sorrow by reason of its great sin.[1]

Methodism emphasized what we call "experiential religion." Something happened that men and women *felt*. They knew for themselves that there is a God and that he forgives sins, accepts the sinner, and makes him his child. They knew this because it happened to them. Salvation, they found, was not

[1] H. T. Hudson, *The Methodist Armor.*

something read of in a book, nor preached from a pulpit—
it was something lived in life and known as immediate, firsthand experience. They meant it when they sang:

> O how happy are they
> Who the Saviour obey,
> And have laid up their treasure above!
> Tongue can never express
> The sweet comfort and peace
> Of a soul in its earliest love.

Every Methodist was expected to have some sort of Christian
experience, something he could be sure of, something he
could tell to others.

These first Methodists were not happy unless and until they
were telling others of God and of what he had done for them.
So the "experience meeting" came to be a feature of many
early Methodist gatherings. In such meetings and elsewhere the
account of those who had found God stirred others, and they
in turn stirred others. The revival rolled on.

By the genius of its leader, John Wesley, and by the systematic way the societies worked and worshiped, the Methodist revival began early to express itself in definite patterns of
activity. So class meetings, love feasts, conferences, came into
being—also stewards, class leaders, and an itinerant ministry—
that is, a moving and traveling one. A well-integrated organization—though not as yet a separate Church—began to take
shape as each new duty or emergency called for some action
or plan to meet it.

The Methodist idea of church organization has always been
that the power of the divine Spirit will express itself through
whatever forms are needed to perpetuate and spread the gospel, and that the church itself must be flexible enough in its

orders and processes to follow wherever the Spirit seems to lead. Every true church must be constantly making adjustments to new challenges and new situations, keeping always the solid, sure, scriptural basis of the Christian life.

Within ten years after the start of the United Societies of Methodism in England, the outlines of the future Church were becoming visible and the patterns of its organization taking shape. There was then no idea that there would be a Methodist Church, for all were loyal members of the Church of England. Societies formed in separate places, however, were tied to one another in what Methodists then and now speak of as a "connection." Quarterly meetings in each local church were held, and business was transacted much as in our present Quarterly Conferences. Annual meetings of the preachers soon became known as the Annual Conference. A preaching ministry thus came about, with men speaking and witnessing and traveling according to a uniform system. So Methodism was off on its glorious career.

JOHN WESLEY, THE FOUNDER

was one of the most remarkable men who ever lived. He combined great energy and organizing ability with religious genius of the highest order.

He was born in Epworth parsonage in Lincolnshire, England, in 1703. His father, Samuel Wesley, was a clergyman of the Church of England; his mother, Susannah Wesley, was one of the great mothers of men. Pious, cultured, and strict, she brought up her large family of children according to exact religious rules of everyday living. The Epworth parsonage in its rigorous discipline became the cradle of Methodism. A great many Methodist rules for sincere Christian living had their origin at Epworth. To this background of a devoted home Wesley added the distinction of becoming one of the most famous graduates of Oxford University. While at Oxford he decided to become a clergyman of the Church and in due time was ordained as such. He was tremendously in earnest in his religious life, and with the other members of the Holy Club he spent his time in doing good "over and above the call of duty." He visited the jail inmates, ministered to the poor, attended Communion services regularly.

However, in all this John Wesley was not happy—he felt that there should be a joy and peace in religion which he did not have. Then he decided to go to America and help convert the Indians in the newly opened province of Georgia. Charles Wesley, his brother, had been made secretary to General Oglethorpe, who was in charge of the Georgia colony. So the Wesley brothers sailed for Savannah, where John Wesley spent some months as rector of the Savannah church. But his ministry was neither happy nor successful, and he went back to England. There, still seeking to find God, he had an experience which changed his whole life.

While sitting in a prayer meeting in an Aldersgate Street house in London with a small company of Christians, he said that he felt his heart "strangely warmed." "I felt I did trust in Christ, Christ alone for salvation; and an assurance was given me that he had taken away my sins, even mine, and saved me from the law of sin and death."

From that minute John Wesley was a changed man. Before his "conversion," as we call it, he knew what religion was theoretically; afterward he knew practically—or, as we say, experientially. No longer was it what the books had said or what the church lecturers had maintained, but what he himself *knew*. And what Wesley found that God could do for him, he knew God could do for others—and he began to preach it with might and main.

From that time on John Wesley was a man full of power

and of the Holy Spirit. His intellectual faculties were greatly kindled, his spiritual wisdom grew, and his energy knew no bounds. Soon he began to travel and to preach and to organize into societies, or bands, all who were converted. A vast and growing spiritual movement took place under his leadership. England soon began to ring with the Methodist revival.

Wesley did two things which greatly magnified the power and force of Methodism: (1) he created a corps of lay preachers (local preachers, we would call them), who gave all the time they could to preaching under his direction; (2) he adopted outdoor, or field, preaching in a big way. This was simply preaching out of doors in any convenient place—in a meadow, a vacant city lot, on the steps of a building, anywhere. In this way Wesley and his preachers took the gospel to those who otherwise never would have heard it.

Methodist preachers soon were seen going everywhere. They held their meetings wherever they could get people to listen, while men and women who had been converted backed them up by telling publicly how God had changed their lives. Crowds flocked to hear, and the revival grew apace. Singing was heard—such singing as England never had known before. Charles Wesley, the brother of John, began to write hymns, as did others; and the enthusiastic chorus of outdoor multitudes awakened England, Wales, Scotland, and North Ireland. Everywhere people who had been dead to religion found happiness and purpose in life and in turn told others.

But all was not smooth sailing. The regular clergy of the Church of England, especially the bishops, frowned on all such irregular goings on. They called it "enthusiasm" and would have none of it. The Bishop of Bristol told John Wesley that he was not commissioned to preach in his diocese and had no business there. Wesley replied that his business on earth was to do what good he could and "woe is me if I preach not the gospel wherever I am in the habitable world."

To another clergyman critical on the same point Wesley gave the historic reply that Methodism has nailed to her masthead ever since: "I look upon all the world as my parish."

For some years there was active hostility to the movement and some real persecution. Mobs in several places broke up the Methodist outdoor meetings with sticks and stones. Wesley himself was stoned and mobbed several times, and one or two of his preachers were killed. But God was in the revival, and it kept spreading. Bad men became good; drunkards became sober; religion wrote itself in changed lives everywhere, and this could not be denied. Wesley lived to see Methodism established widely over the English-speaking world; and when he died, full of years and of honor, he could say sincerely, "The best of all is, God is with us."

American Methodism

Methodism, which swept through England, in time crossed the Atlantic and was destined to influence tremendously the whole American continent.

The first American society was organized in New York by Philip Embury, a local preacher. He was prompted to do this by his cousin Barbara Heck, a Christian woman who had become greatly concerned over the worldliness which seemed to be engulfing them all. Embury and Barbara Heck were emigrants from Ireland and were originally of German stock. Embury had been a preacher for a time in Ireland. As the story goes, one day Barbara Heck came in and found a card game in progress. With a sudden defiant move she seized the cards, threw them into the fire, and whirled on Embury: "Philip, if you don't preach to us, we will all go to hell."

Embury, aroused in conscience because he knew that he had

17

been neglectful, began to preach and exhort. A small society was started. A British army officer named Captain Webb, a man of some means, shortly after joined the group; and in 1768 the first Methodist chapel was built on John Street, New York. The John Street Church still stands today amid the skyscrapers of the Wall Street district. Two brass candlesticks which Dame Barbara brought to "meeting" and then took home afterward now are standing squarely on either side of the John Street pulpit—fit emblems of an indomitable woman.

At about the same time that John Street was started, an Irish emigrant named Robert Strawbridge built a Methodist log chapel at Sam's Creek in Maryland. Here began another Methodist group destined to live and grow. The John Street society consisted of but fifty persons a few years after its founding; Strawbridge's log meetinghouse did not have that large a following. But the power of God was with them; and "as green forests sleep in the tiny cup of acorns, so grand possibilities slumbered in this mustard seed of vital religion."

In 1769 Richard Boardman and Joseph Pilmoor, the first itinerant preachers sent by Wesley to "American circuit," arrived. Boardman was stationed at John Street in New York, Pilmoor as pastor in Philadelphia.

Two years later, in 1771, Wesley sent to America FRANCIS ASBURY, a man who was destined under God to influence and shape the growing Methodist connection in America more than any other man. Asbury was but a youth when he arrived but within a few years, and thereafter until his death in 1816, was the acknowledged and undisputed leader of the whole connection in America.

In 1773 the first Annual Conference was held at Philadelphia. There were ten preachers present—Thomas Rankin, Richard Boardman, Joseph Pilmoor, Francis Asbury, Richard

Wright, George Shadford, Thomas Webb, John King, A. Whitworth, Joseph Yearbry—names which remain in Methodist history as do those of the signers of the Declaration of Independence in national annals. These men looked after 6 circuits and 1,160 members.

Meanwhile Methodism spread to the South, where in Maryland and Virginia it was destined to have marvelous growth. In 1774 Robert Williams began to organize societies in Virginia, and two years later farther south the "Carolina" Circuit came into being. Williams was a rousing preacher, always on the move with the true evangelist's zeal of getting things done at once. Virginia and Carolina Methodists both can look back to Robert Williams as their spiritual father. Although the American Revolution broke with full fury on these colonies in 1777-78, yet even during its dark and bitter days great revivals were held in the tidewater country of Virginia and North Carolina. Eighteen hundred souls were added to these societies in one year.

But the Methodist congregations, which called themselves societies as long as the colonies belonged to England, had to become a Church after America was free. For the Church of England (to which most of the Methodists looked for ordained clergymen to give them the sacraments) had, of course, gone with the withdrawal of English rule. The Methodists in the United States thereupon felt compelled, and indeed were glad, to unite into a church, which should be thereafter a self-governing, independent, Christian Church, to the glory of God and the advancement of his kingdom.

Organization of the Church

The METHODIST EPISCOPAL CHURCH was formally organized at a conference of Methodist ministers in Baltimore in the last week of December, 1784. Famous in Methodist annals as the Christmas Conference (as it began December 25 and lasted until Janunary 2, 1785), this organization meeting put its stamp upon all subsequent actions and the entire future development of Methodism in America.

It adopted a name, The Methodist Episcopal Church. This indicated that the church should be Methodist in its doctrine and discipline; and Episcopal, that is, organized under bishops, in its form of church government.

The Christmas Conference also adopted a prayer book known as the *Sunday Service,* sent over by John Wesley. This contained the Articles of Religion, which the present church still holds (see page 26), and also directed the manner of conducting worship, especially in the sacramental services, marriage, burial, and so on. As the *Sunday Service* was an abridgment of the *Book of Common Prayer* of the Church of England, this accounts for the similarity between our Methodist worship and ritual and that of the Church of England and the Protestant Episcopal Church in America.

The Christmas Conference also elected two men as bishops for the Methodist Episcopal Church—Francis Asbury and Thomas Coke. These, the first Methodist bishops, were at first called superintendents; but in a few years the title was changed to Bishop.

Twelve other men were elected "elders" by the Christmas Conference, ordained to be ministers and empowered to administer Communion. Up to that time Methodist preachers had been simply "preachers" and had no right to administer the sacraments. They were viewed as laymen who went about preaching in a sort of irregular way. But at the Christmas Conference and afterward men were ordained into the ministry of the Methodist Episcopal Church; and their orders—that is, their ministerial status—were never questioned by any except a few high-church persons who felt that no one could be rightly ordained except by an English bishop. Today the validity of Methodist orders is generally recognized over the entire church world.

It is necessary to describe rather fully the Christmas Conference of 1784, for in importance it outranks all subsequent general church gatherings. While Methodism had its roots deep in the established Church of England and in the historic church of the past, and while it can claim an unbroken chain of ordinations and of churchly practice reaching far back, yet the Christmas Conference truly gave to the world a new church. That church was destined to increase and multiply at first by tens of thousands, then by hundreds of thousands, and now by millions; and, please God, it shall continue so long as it can and will carry out the will of God.

An old history of New Jersey, when surveying the religious life of that state, says rather dryly: "The Methodists got started about the time of the Revolution, but after it, for the next fifty years, Methodism like a great wave rolled over Jersey." It rolled over all the colonies, then over the states, then across the passes in the Appalachians to the Mississippi, the western plains, and on to the shores of the Pacific. Growth was marvelous. By 1796 there were 56,664 members; by 1806, 130,570; in 1826, 360,800; in 1836, 650,103; at the time of the Civil War 1,032,184.[2] That war interrupted life greatly, especially in the South; and Methodism lost thousands, but in a few years regained its power and went ahead. Annual Conference after Annual Conference was organized as the church grew and as the American people themselves multiplied.

The Methodist Church was peculiarly suited to the American scene, whether it was the frontier or the crowded city; it is suited to the American temperament, which it has always expressed and embodied in all its actions and viewpoints. Both

[2] Abel Stevens, *A Compendious History of American Methodism.*

preachers and people have been part and parcel of the nation itself. The big Methodist faults—and we have them, let us confess—are the big American faults; and the big Methodist virtues—and, thank God, we have them too—are the big American virtues. Our church is in fact not only the largest but the most evenly distributed Protestant church in the United States. When Theodore Roosevelt was President, he once privately remarked to the chaplain of the United States Senate, who was a Methodist, "Your church is the church of America."

Alongside the great growth in numbers went a vast development in all other areas of church life. Missions to foreign lands as well as those at home were started early in the nineteenth century. Melville Cox, the first native American missionary, went to Africa, other brave pioneers to India. Soon the spreading sails of moving ships were taking men and women from our shores to the ends of the earth, while the home churches supported them with money and with prayers. Stories began to come back—stories of success almost apostolic—together with insistent calls for more men and more money. Liberally the home conferences responded until the far-flung empire of Methodist missions was flying its flag over fifty-five nations of the earth.

Schools and colleges were built, keeping pace with the growth of the church. Beginning with Cokesbury College at Abingdon, Maryland, other institutions were added—academies, seminaries, colleges, universities—until today the Board of Education has under its charge or directly related to it many nationally known institutions of higher learning and all kinds of secondary schools, training centers, and the like.

Orphanages and homes for the needy, the aged, and the infirm soon were erected by the growing church. To take care of the fatherless and the widows and to help the sick and the afflicted has always been a Christian goal. Methodism is proud of the assertion once made regarding it that it is "Christianity in earnest."

Time would fail to tell of the other great works of The Methodist Church though some of these will be referred to later in this book. Enough has been said to indicate that the church grew not only in numbers but in its effective outreach to mankind. The Methodist *Discipline* truly states that the message of the Church shall always have a double emphasis:

First is the gospel of God's grace, offered to all men and equal to every human need.

Second is the moral ideal which this gospel presents to men.

Toward the fulfilling of these ideal purposes The Methodist Church has not been behind in any generation.

In its growth the Methodist Episcopal Church in the United States was divided a number of times. A list of all these divisions and the reasons for them would take too much space here, but two were of high importance. One was the withdrawal in 1828 of Methodists who called for greater lay rights in the church and who subsequently organized the Methodist Protestant Church. This church had a long and honored history, and its members lived to see the Methodist Episcopal churches adopt the principle of lay representation which the original Methodist Protestants had withdrawn to secure. The Methodists Protestants joined in the great move for Methodist union in 1939 and played a big part in consummating it.

In 1844 the original Methodist Episcopal Church divided, and the Methodist Episcopal Church, South, was organized. The reasons for this epochal separation were variously interpreted by representatives of the two sections. Northern Methodists claimed it was due to the South's holding onto slavery; southern Methodists claimed it was over the question as to the power of the General Conference over a bishop. A vast sectional cleavage was behind the division, and the Civil War soon proved how far apart men in the same church might be when it came to social and political questions. Happily, after the long years had healed the hurt of war and allayed the fierce antagonisms of earlier days, the two churches came together in an unbreakable union in 1939 and with the Methodist Protestant Church formed THE METHODIST CHURCH. That church, now vast in extent and great in numbers, is still writing its own history.

CHAPTER TWO

Doctrine and Beliefs

THE METHODIST CHURCH is a Christian church standing squarely on the Bible for its doctrine and belief. It is a Protestant church. It holds to the essential truths of pure Christianity as re-emphasized in the Protestant Reformation when Martin Luther and other Protestant reformers broke with the Church of Rome in the sixteenth century.

Methodist beliefs are embodied and expressed in a terse, concrete way in the Apostles' Creed. "Methodism is settled in the apostolic theology," affirmed Bishop Horace M. DuBose in *The Symbol of Methodism*. "The Apostles' Creed . . . is its Creed." This creed, or affirmation of faith, Methodists are expected to repeat Sunday after Sunday as part of their worship. Methodist standards of doctrine are more definitely stated in

TWENTY-FIVE ARTICLES OF RELIGION

FIFTY-TWO SERMONS OF JOHN WESLEY, and

NOTES ON THE NEW TESTAMENT BY JOHN WESLEY

These three, the Articles, the Sermons, and the Notes are commonly taken as the Methodist standards of doctrine. As the fifty-two sermons (which Wesley selected as containing the doctrines he held); and his *Notes on the New Testament* are difficult to boil down, American Methodists usually take the Articles of Religion as the concrete expression of their belief. Where there may be a question as to the meaning of an Article

or its specific interpretation, they refer back to the teaching
or preaching of Wesley or the early Methodist preachers to
settle the matter.

Methodists have never been too doctrinally conscious. They
"lead with their hearts instead of their heads," a popular mag-
azine has said of them.[1] The practical living of the Christian
life has always meant more to Methodists than hair-splitting
theological discussions. "Is thine heart right as my heart is with
thy heart?" Wesley was accustomed to ask when men wanted
to argue with him over matters of doctrine. "If it is, give me
thy hand." Another time he explained, "In opinions that do
not strike at the root of Christianity, we Methodists think and
let think."

The bishops of the church in addressing the General Conference of 1952 put it thus: "Our theology has never been a
closely organized doctrinal system. We have never insisted on
uniformity of thought or statement." Heresy trials are therefore practically unknown among Methodists. If a person wants
to live a Christian life and affirms that he sincerely accepts
Jesus Christ as Saviour and Lord, that is enough. Nevertheless
it is entirely incorrect to say that Methodism has no formal
doctrine. "There are great Christian doctrines which we most
surely hold and most firmly believe," said the bishops in the
address referred to above. Methodism is undergirded with profound convictions regarding the important verities of the New
Testament faith.

Specifically the church has an august framework of belief
in its twenty-five

ARTICLES OF RELIGION

These articles were selected by John Wesley from the Thirty-
nine Articles of the Church of England and sent to American

[1] "Methodists: Stock Taking." *Newsweek*, May 10, 1948, p. 70.

Methodism. The Methodist Episcopal Church at its beginning adopted these articles as setting forth its faith, and to this day The Methodist Church publishes them in its *Discipline,* and they are part of the Constitution of the Church.

No Methodist or group of Methodists, not even the General Conference of the church, has a right to change any of the articles even by a word. These historic affirmations of faith can be altered only by a long-drawn-out process of amending the constitution. This requires four years to effect and the all-but-unanimous consent of the whole church acting together.

In the succeeding pages of this chapter I shall take up the Articles of Religion in order. I will show how they are each based on Bible truth and then will endeavor to make clear in modern language their underlying meaning.

The interpretation here given will be as nearly as possible that of John Wesley and the Methodist theologians up to and through the nineteenth century. Admittedly present-day Methodist theologians differ from one another in some matters of doctrinal interpretation, and in some respects from traditional Methodist positions. Their right to do so is allowable under the liberty that Christian men have—as Wesley would put it—to "think and let think." Indeed no faith could grow were there no possibility of restating its truths in the thought forms which each new age demands.

Differing modern interpretations, however, do not provide an authoritative standard or even a definite one, and surely when it comes to the standards of doctrine of a great Christian Church, there ought to be a unified, forthright approach, not a divided one. Since it would not be fair to all Methodists to take one particular modern school of thought as definitive, in the following pages are set forth the traditional Methodist teaching as this was almost invariably expressed through 150

27

years of Methodist expansion. I find myself in wholehearted agreement with this view.

It is important to realize that each one of the articles was written in answer to a direct question or a direct challenge to some point of faith. Certain articles, for instance, were to answer infidels or agnostics who wanted to know what the church believed about God and Christ; some were to refute Roman Catholic teachings about the sacraments or worship of saints, and so on; some were to answer Calvinists and their teachings. The fact that the articles came about in answer to special challenges explains why they do not cover *everything* a Christian may believe.

It also explains the ancient phraseology of the articles. Some of them spend a considerable time on issues no longer alive or of great interest to modern Christians. Nevertheless the Articles of Religion do set forth in a powerful, if somewhat stilted, way the main tenets of the Christian faith as The Methodist Church officially holds them. "The Articles of Religion," affirmed Bishop Holland N. McTyeire, "together with the 'established standards of doctrine,' make a system as complete as it is orthodox." [2]

The Articles of Religion are as follows:

1. Of Faith in the Holy Trinity

There is but one living and true God, everlasting, without body or parts, of infinite power, wisdom, and goodness; the maker and preserver of all things, visible and invisible. And in unity of this Godhead there are three persons, of one substance, power, and eternity— the Father, the Son, and the Holy Ghost.

[2] Hudson, *op. cit.*

28

SCRIPTURAL BASIS:[3] "Hear, O Israel: the Lord our God is one Lord." (Deut. 6:4.) "Thou, even thou, art Lord alone; thou hast made heaven, the heaven of heavens, with all their host, the earth, and all things that are therein, the seas, and all that is therein, and thou preservest them all." (Neh. 9:6.) "Holy, holy, holy, is the Lord of hosts: the whole earth is full of his glory." (Isa. 6:3.) "But the Lord is the true God, he is the living God." (Jer. 10:10.) "From everlasting to everlasting, thou art God." (Ps. 90:2.) "One God and Father of all." (Eph. 4:6.) "God is a Spirit." (John 4:24.) "God is love." (I John 4:16.) "To God only wise, be glory." (Rom. 16:27.) "Now unto the King eternal, immortal, invisible, the only wise God, be honour and glory for ever and ever. Amen." (I Tim. 1:17.)

This, the first of all affirmations of faith, asserts belief in God—God as creator, God as all-powerful, and God as good. All who are not atheists (who do not believe in any god) or agnostics (who say they don't know) can join with us in agreeing to the first part of this article. Jews and Moslems, as well as Christians of all sects, agree about the greatness and power and watch care of God.

God is *one*—so true faith has always insisted against all people, ancient or modern, who worship many gods. That God is a *living* God is asserted against all idol worshipers or those who think God to be a vast cosmic principle that, they suppose, runs the world. Our God is a living Person, whether called Jehovah or Lord or whatever name.

Notice the attributes or characteristics of God. He is *everlasting;* he is *without body or parts*—that is, he is not like the things or people he has created. He is far greater. Also he is a

[3] The scriptural basis cited in connection with this and the other articles is not to be thought of as a resort to prooftexts. Rather it is the endeavor to select and set forth within the framework of orthodox biblical theology the particular affirmations which highlight and emphasize the broader truths which the church has always steadfastly believed.

Spirit, as Jesus told the Samaritan woman (John 4:24). He is infinite in *power,* in *wisdom,* and in *goodness.*

God is good, and God is great—these are the two attributes of God on which Christianity bases its whole theology and on which we rest our complete hope. Even when we pass through the valley of the shadow of death, we fear no evil, resting in the goodness and greatness of God. " *'Infinite* goodness!' " exclaimed a Methodist bishop years ago; " 'the glorious gospel of the blessed God' [is] wrapped up in that matchless phrase." [4]

2. Of the Word, or Son of God, Who Was Made Very Man

The Son, who is the Word of the Father, the very and eternal God, of one substance with the Father, took man's nature in the womb of the blessed Virgin; so that two whole and perfect natures, that is to say, the God-head and Manhood, were joined together in one person, never to be divided; whereof is one Christ, very God and very Man, who truly suffered, was crucified, dead, and buried, to reconcile his Father to us, and to be a sacrifice, not only for original guilt, but also for the actual sins of men.

SCRIPTURAL BASIS: "There is one God, and one mediator between God and men, the man Christ Jesus." (I Tim. 2:5.) "But to us there is but one God, the Father, of whom are all things, and we in him; and one Lord Jesus Christ, by whom are all things, and we by him." (I Cor. 8:6.) "In the beginning was the Word, and the Word was with God and the Word was God." (John 1:1.) "The Word was made flesh, and dwelt among us, (and we beheld his glory, the glory as of the only begotten of the Father,) full of grace and truth." (John 1:14.) "In him dwelleth all the fulness of the Godhead bodily." (Col. 2:9.) "I came forth from the Father, and am come into the world: again, I leave the world, and go to the Father."

[4] H. M. DuBose, *The Symbol of Methodism.*

30

(John 16:28.) "He that hath seen me hath seen the Father." (John 14:9.) "God, having raised up his Son Jesus, sent him to bless you, in turning away every one of you from his iniquities." (Acts 3:26.) "Thou art that Christ, the Son of the living God." (John 6:69.)

This is the first distinctively Christian affirmation of faith. This article sets forth in one long sentence the whole matter of the gospel: that God became man and lived on earth; that Godhood and manhood were joined together in one person, Jesus Christ, who was truly both God and man; and that this Christ was "crucified, dead, and buried" to restore the broken fellowship of God and man, and save men from their sins. This is the gospel. This is the good news. How, or in what manner, Christ effected this is something else; but that it has been done is as clear as sunlight—Christ is our redeemer.

Jews and Moslems believe in God, but Christians believe in Jesus Christ as the divine Son of God. "These are written," John explains as he finishes his whole Gospel, "that ye might believe that Jesus [whose life and deeds he sets forth] *is the Christ*, . . . and that believing ye might have life through his name." (20:31.) Christianity is Christ.

3. Of the Resurrection of Christ

Christ did truly rise again from the dead, and took again his body, with all things appertaining to the perfection of man's nature, wherewith he ascended into heaven, and there sitteth until he return to judge all men at the last day.

SCRIPTURAL BASIS: All the Gospels tell of the Resurrection in detail. "Go quickly and tell his disciples that he is risen from the dead." (Matt. 28:7.) "But now is Christ risen from the dead, and become the firstfruits of them that slept." (I Cor. 15:20.)

Ascension and Session: "While they beheld, he was taken up; and a cloud received him." (Acts 1:9.) "This same Jesus, which is taken up from you into heaven, shall so come in like manner as ye have seen him go into heaven." (Acts 1:11.) "So then after the Lord had spoken unto them, he was received up into heaven, and sat on the right hand of God." (Mark 16:19.) "It is Christ that died, yea rather, that is risen again, who is even at the right hand of God, who also maketh intercession for us." (Rom. 8:34.) "When [God] raised him from the dead, and set him at his own right hand in the heavenly places." (Eph. 1:20.) "This man, after he had offered one sacrifice for sins for ever, sat down on the right hand of God." (Heb. 10:12.)

Second Advent and Judgment: "If I go and prepare a place for you, I will come again, and receive you unto myself." (John 14:3.) "Our conversation is in heaven; from whence also we look for the Saviour, the Lord Jesus Christ." (Phil. 3:20.) "Whom the heavens must receive until the times of restitution of all things." (Acts. 3:21.) "When the Lord Jesus shall be revealed from heaven with his mighty angels." (II Thess. 1:7.) "[God] hath appointed a day, in which he will judge the world in righteousness by that man whom he hath ordained; whereof he hath given assurance unto all men, in that he hath raised him from the dead." (Acts 17:31.) "For the Father judgeth no man, but hath committed all judgment unto the Son." (John 5:22.)

The resurrection of Christ, as affirmed in Article 3, was the seal and confirmation of all Jesus' teachings, of all that he had said of himself. When Christ rose from the dead, he not only certified to the truth of all that had been believed regarding him, but started a new order of beings in the universe of God. He was, as the apostle Paul said, the "firstfruits of them that slept." That is, by being the first to rise among all those who had died since time began, he assumed first place in the new order of God.

Christianity may yield on other points, but it cannot yield on the Resurrection. Our hope and our faith are based on it. There was no pretense, no lively imagination, no purely ethereal appearance. *"Five* times he showed himself alive" on the day of his resurection—"to Mary Magdalene, to another company of women, to Peter, to two disciples on their way to Emmaus, to the eleven; to St. Thomas in the prayer-meeting; then in Galilee; to seven, and to five hundred. They knew him by many infallible proofs." [5]

Christianity is the religion of a great hope. Christ's was the first of all the graves that shall finally be opened when he shall have "put all enemies under his feet."

The last affirmation of this article has to do with the ascension of Christ, his session, and his second coming to judge the earth. The account of the Ascension and promise that the Lord shall come again is found in the first chapter of the Acts of the Apostles. The Ascension marked the end of the earthly life of Jesus but in no way ended the spiritual presence of the living Christ. He is our eternal contemporary, known to all who truly live in him.

The Session, or sitting of Christ at the right hand of God, is a symbolic way of representing the fact that all power belongs to Christ both in heaven and on earth.

The final return of Christ to judge the quick and the dead—the Second Coming, or Second Advent—is affirmed in this article, as it is in the Apostles' Creed. An eager expectation of the Lord's return is reflected at many places in the New Testament. But neither this article nor the creed undertakes to tell *when* the Lord shall return, and he himself said that he did not know (Mark 13:32). Because of the vagaries and wild prophecies of Adventist groups, and controversies between premillennialists and postmillennialists, many pres-

[5] Hudson, *op. cit.*

ent-day Christians have a tendency to ignore, and some to rebel against, the whole idea of a Second Advent. Practical Christians, including most Methodists, usually take the position that since we cannot know and are not meant to know about "times and seasons," we should get on with our own daily lives and leave the rest to God. But it is undeniable that the New Testament does teach that the Lord shall return in God's own time, and this to many thoughtful Christians is the

> One far-off divine event,
> To which the whole creation moves.

4. Of the Holy Ghost

The Holy Ghost, proceeding from the Father and the Son, is of one substance, majesty, and glory, with the Father and the Son, very and eternal God.

SCRIPTURAL BASIS: "Baptizing them in the name of the Father, and of the Son, and of the Holy Ghost." (Matt. 28:19.) "When he, the Spirit of truth, is come, he will guide you into all truth." (John 16:13.) "The Spirit itself beareth witness with our spirit, that we are the children of God." (Rom. 8:16.) "Holy men of God spake as they were moved by the Holy Ghost." (II Pet. 1:21.) "And they were all filled with the Holy Ghost." (Acts 2:4.) "The Lord is that Spirit." (II Cor. 3:17.)

Our faith teaches that there is one God, but that he exists in three persons—God the Father, God the Son, and God the Holy Spirit. The Father is not the Son, nor the Holy Spirit, but is God. The Son is not the Father and not the Holy Spirit, but is God. The Holy Spirit is not the Father and not the Son, but is God. And this triune God, or God in three persons, is a "blessed Trinity," as a familiar hymn

34

expresses it. "God Himself is the Father revealed; God Himself is in Christ revealing; God Himself is the Holy Spirit abiding."

The human mind cannot fathom the exact relationship of God within himself, and for ages men have asked how three can be one and not three. But to all this the heart has an answer which words can never completely express: whoever knows God, feels his Spirit and loves his Son, and is at peace in the Father's keeping.

The coming of the Holy Ghost, or the divine Comforter, at Pentecost marked the definite beginning of the new Dispensation. (Acts 2:4.) Pentecost was the name of a Jewish festival day, fifty days after the Passover. But in the Christian calendar it became the birthday of the Church.

Before that day came, the small band of disciples were timid and afraid. They met secretly behind closed doors "for fear of the Jews." They seemed to be waiting for something; as indeed they were, for they had been promised "power from on high." That power was given on the day of Pentecost when the Holy Spirit came upon the disciples. Immediately everything changed. No more were there secret meetings in closed upper rooms. The lambs had become lions, and Peter stood out on the street and preached with tremendous courage and boldness. The Holy Spirit had come to be with God's own forever.

That Spirit still continues to lead and guide and will always direct the people who are his. Belief in the Holy Spirit is belief not in the dead past but in the living present and the glorious future, for he continues to show us "things to come." William F. Warren's great hymn puts it:

> I worship Thee, O Holy Ghost,
>   I love to worship Thee;
> With Thee each day is Pentecost,
>   Each night Nativity.

5. Of the Sufficiency of the Holy Scriptures for Salvation

The Holy Scriptures contain all things necessary to salvation; so that whatsoever is not read therein, nor may be proved thereby, is not to be required of any man that it should be believed as an article of faith, or be thought requisite or necessary to salvation. In the name of the Holy Scriptures we do understand those canonical books of the Old and New Testament of whose authority was never any doubt in the Church. The names of the canonical books are:

Genesis, Exodus, Leviticus, Numbers, Deuteronomy, Joshua, Judges, Ruth, The First Book of Samuel, The Second Book of Samuel, The First Book of Kings, The Second Book of Kings, The First Book of Chronicles, The Second Book of Chronicles, The Book of Ezra, The Book of Nehemiah, The Book of Esther, The Book of Job, The Psalms, The Proverbs, Ecclesiastes or the Preacher, Cantica or Song of Solomon, Four Prophets the Greater, Twelve Prophets the Less.

All the books of the New Testament, as they are commonly received, we do receive and account canonical.

SCRIPTURAL BASIS: "The law of the Lord is perfect, converting the soul: the testimony of the Lord is sure, making wise the simple." (Ps. 19:7.) "Search the scriptures; for in them ye think ye have eternal life: and they are they which testify of me." (John 5:39.) "From a child thou hast known the holy scriptures, which are able to make thee wise unto salvation." (II Tim. 3:15.) "And receive with meekness the engrafted word, which is able to save your souls." (Jas. 1:21.) "And beginning at Moses and all the prophets, he [Jesus] expounded unto them in all the scriptures the things concerning himself." (Luke 24:27.)

The first sentence of this article is the bedrock of Protestantism. The Bible contains *all things necessary to salvation.* That is the prime affirmation. The Bible contains all sorts of other things also, let us admit—history, philosophy, poetry, wisdom, law—and a reverent scholarship can help greatly in understanding and explaining all these. But through all the study of expositors and interpreters, believers or unbelievers, the Bible stands exactly where this article of our faith says it does, as the one writing containing all things needful to a person's salvation. As salvation depends upon Christ, so Christians believe that the purpose of all scripture from Genesis to the final word in Revelation is to lead us to Christ. As Mary Lathbury's hymn puts it:

> Beyond the sacred page
> I seek Thee, Lord;
> My spirit pants for Thee,
> O living Word!

Further, whatsoever is not read in the Bible or cannot be proved by it is not to be required of any man as something to be believed. This part of the article sweeps away all the traditions of men and makes the rules of churches and of councils and of popes unnecessary. The Roman Catholic Church, for instance, has established many rules and customs not found in scripture. The encyclicals of the popes fill eight volumes; the acts of church councils fill ninety; all sorts of procedures—the worship of saints, worship of relics, masses and prayers for the dead, for instance—are taught by that church as binding upon belief. Indeed, the Council of Trent decreed that all these traditions, written and unwritten, should be of equal authority with the Bible, "and that he that denies it shall be accursed." But Methodism, with all Protestantism, does deny this flatly. *If it is not in the Bible, it does not have to be believed.*

6. Of the Old Testament

The Old Testament is not contrary to the New; for both in the Old and New Testament everlasting life is offered to mankind by Christ, who is the only Mediator between God and man, being both God and Man. Wherefore they are not to be heard who feign that the old fathers did look only for transitory promises. Although the law given from God by Moses as touching ceremonies and rites doth not bind Christians, nor ought the civil precepts thereof of necessity be received in any commonwealth; yet notwithstanding, no Christian whatsoever is free from the obedience of the commandments which are called moral.

SCRIPTURAL BASIS: "Beginning at Moses and all the prophets, he expounded unto them in all the scriptures the things concerning himself. . . . And he said unto them, These are the words which I spake unto you, while I was yet with you, that all things must be fulfilled, which were written in the law of Moses, and in the prophets, and in the psalms, concerning me." (Luke 24:27, 44.) "Think not that I am come to destroy the law, or the prophets: I am not come to destroy, but to fulfil." (Matt. 5:17.)

The Old Testament is not contrary to the New. The whole Bible is here treated as a unified revelation. We are Christians, but we are heirs also of all God's promises. God, who spoke by the prophets (the Old Testament), finally spoke by his Son (the New Testament). It is a mistake, as this article teaches, to discount what the Old Testament promises. Christ himself is said to have made ninety quotations from the Old Testament to support his teachings. When tempted of the devil, his great weapon was, "*It is written.*" The prophets and seers were forerunners for us. "In the Old Testament the New lies hidden: in the New, the Old stands revealed."

The Church of Christ cannot afford to forget these truths. Nevertheless, as this article affirms, Christians are not bound by all the minute regulations, the rites and ceremonies, of the law as given by Moses. Christ did away with the ceremonial law; and his people are saved by faith, not by works. But we do admit that the "commandments which are called moral," as the last line of this article insists, are binding upon all Christians.

What are the moral commandments? They are taken to comprise the Ten Commandments, as well as the deep natural principles written in the hearts of honest and just people everywhere. Even the heathen, as Paul expressed it, "do by nature the things contained in the law" (Rom. 2:14).

7. Of Original or Birth Sin

Original sin standeth not in the following of Adam (as the Pelagians do vainly talk), but it is the corruption of the nature of every man, that naturally is engendered of the offspring of Adam, whereby man is very far gone from original righteousness, and of his own nature inclined to evil, and that continually.

SCRIPTURAL BASIS: "By one man sin entered into the world, and death by sin; and so death passed upon all men, for that all have sinned." (Rom. 5:12.) "By one man's disobedience many were made sinners." (Rom. 5:19.)

The medieval Church, the Puritans, and certain others have insisted that every child is "conceived and born in sin." Nothing can be further from the whole drift and drive of the religion of Jesus. "Suffer the little children to come unto me, and forbid them not: for of such is the kingdom of God" (Mark 10:14.) And again, "Except ye . . . become as little children, ye shall not enter into the kingdom of heaven"

(Matt. 18:3). Marriage is a holy estate; and each newborn babe comes fresh-minted, as it were, from the hand of God, bearing the impress and image of the Creator. But—and here is the practical truth that was in the mind of those who wrote this article—in time everyone, no matter how pure at birth, finds within himself a powerful bent toward evil. "Of his own nature *inclined* to evil, and that continually," the article puts it.

This is sadly true. No matter how it got into man, a moral pull downward is always present. Why is this—the "corruption . . . that naturally is engendered of the offspring of Adam, whereby man is very far gone from original righteousness"? Certainly it is something that all men seem to have unfailingly inherited.

Leaving aside all theory, what we know from universal experience is that "all have sinned, and come short of the glory of God" and all do need a Saviour. The way out—salvation—is not to "do what comes naturally," but to control and discipline both acts and thoughts that these may be turned upward toward God.

Education and the constant, unremitting teaching of the home, the school, and the church help. Yet with all this something more is needed. "Ye must be born again," said Jesus. And you *must*. For just as there is a physical birth by which all are born into the world, so there is a spiritual birth—whether in a moment or through years, whether conscious or unconscious—by which men and women are born within the spiritual kingdom.

"You cannot trust human nature," is often said. It would be more accurate to say you cannot trust *unredeemed* human nature. For human nature that is redeemed and reflects on earth the Christian virtues of love, peace, joy, long-suffering, temperance, meekness, forbearance—the angels cannot surpass *that*. Temptation will be present as long as we live, but Christ can "take away our bent to sinning" and in place of the downward pull implant in us the upward leading of the divine Spirit.

8. Of Free Will

The condition of man after the fall of Adam is such that he cannot turn and prepare himself, by his own natural strength and works, to faith, and calling upon God; wherefore we have no power to do good works, pleasant and acceptable to God, without the grace of God by Christ preventing us, that we may have a good will, and working with us, when we have that good will.

SCRIPTURAL BASIS: "I am the vine, ye are the branches: He that abideth in me, and I in him, the same bringeth forth much fruit: for without me ye can do nothing." (John 15:5.) "For when we were yet without strength, in due time Christ died for the ungodly." (Rom. 5:6:) "You hath he quickened, who were dead in trespasses and sins." (Eph. 2:1.) "For it is God which worketh in you both to will and to do of his good pleasure." (Phil. 2:13.)

This statement has to do with man's power to find God, or to work his way into a right position with God, *by himself*. This article holds that no man can ever do this *unless* the grace of Christ shall "go ahead of him" (as "prevent" here means).

In other words the gist of this article, its practical value for us today, is that we can't find God unless he first finds us. Man cannot storm the gates of heaven or break in by his own might; he must wait and pray and strive, and so let God find him—as God always does find the sincere seeker. "I would not now be seeking Thee, if I had not already been found of Thee," Pascal beautifully expressed it.

41

The last half of this article opens up the question: Can a bad man do any good at all? Can a non-Christian perform an act pleasing to God? This article taken literally seems to say "no," but not all Christians are this positive. For one thing no one can be sure exactly how God will measure the acts of individual men; also there is a sense in which a good deed, like a gold coin, stands clear in its own right having an inherent value of its own. "It can't be wrong to do right," Robertson of Brighton once said.

Conceivably the grace of God can work in those who have never heard of the gospel. Our Lord taught that there are many who will "come from the east and west" to the judgment of God. That is, there will be unknown pagans who will take their places in God's kingdom because they have done justly and loved mercy. Good deeds alone, all admit, do not suffice; but good deeds are acceptable and pleasing in their own degree.

9. Of the Justification of Man

We are accounted righteous before God only for the merit of our Lord and Saviour Jesus Christ, by faith, and not for our own works or deservings. Wherefore, that we are justified by faith only is a most wholesome doctrine, and very full of comfort.

SCRIPTURAL BASIS: "For by grace are ye saved through faith; and that not of yourselves: it is the gift of God: not of works, lest any man should boast." (Eph. 2:8-9.) "Therefore we conclude that a man is justified by faith without the deeds of the law." (Rom. 3:28.) "Being justified by faith, we have peace with God through our Lord Jesus Christ." (Rom. 5.1.)

This is the great affirmation of Protestantism: JUSTIFICA-TION BY FAITH. It means that we are justified—that is, made right—by God's grace and not by what we do. Paul emphasized this truth again and again in his letters.

The free, spontaneous love of God is what underlies and starts everything in getting men right with God. "God so loved the world, that he gave his only begotten Son, that whosoever *believeth* in him should not perish, but have everlasting life." For a Christian all righteousness is found *through* and *in* Jesus Christ. He has taken away the "handwriting . . . that was against us, . . . nailing it to his cross" (Col. 2:14).

Personal faith, which means personal trust, is the lever here. "Being justified by *faith*, we have peace with God." Faith is the hand extended to receive God's gift. First God offers, then we believe, then we accept. "By grace are ye saved through faith; and that not of yourselves: it is the gift of God." (Eph. 2:8.) If our salvation depended on what we did, how far from it we would be! But as it depends on *what God does,* and what we believe he *can* do, that we are justified by faith becomes, in the quaint language of this article, a "most wholesome doctrine, and very full of comfort."

10. Of Good Works

Although good works, which are the fruits of faith, and follow after justification, cannot put away our sins, and endure the severity of God's judgment; yet are they pleasing and acceptable to God in Christ, and spring out of a true and lively faith, insomuch that by them a lively faith may be as evidently known as a tree is discerned by its fruit.

SCRIPTURAL BASIS: "By the deeds of the law there shall no flesh be justified in his sight." (Rom. 3:20.) "Not by works of righteousness which we have done, but according to his mercy he saved us." (Tit. 3:5.)

The Bible teaches that faith in Christ is the *ground* of salvation, but that good works are the natural expression of that faith. No one can be saved by what he *does*, but those who are saved will wish to do all the good they can. "A lively faith," this article says, "may be as evidently known as a tree is discerned by its fruit."

The above article is definitely aimed at the Roman Catholic doctrine that good works have atoning merit in them. Rome teaches that when men make pilgrimages, go through a course of fasting, say novenas, give donations, or repeat the *Credo* and the Pater Noster, and so on, these things will be put down to their spiritual credit. Protestantism does not so believe. "By works can no man be saved," said Paul. The heart and the spirit must be right irrespective of any or all outward actions, and it takes *Christ* to cleanse hearts and make them pure.

The above article guards against legalism and trusting in external acts. Nevertheless it admits that these outward acts, when they spring from sincere hearts, are well pleasing to God. "Grace in the heart is the fountain, the good works are the streams flowing from it." [6]

Methodists were attacked in earlier days by other Protestants who said that the rules and strict discipline of Methodism were really a sort of salvation-by-works process. This charge was unfounded. No people have ever called for clean hearts and converted lives more than the Methodists; but no people have been more insistent that once having been cleansed in heart and converted in soul by the grace of Christ, the whole of life ought to be so managed and regulated as to bring forth the best and most helpful fruits of faith. We have always taken to heart the command to show our faith by our works.

[6] *Ibid.*

11. Of Works of Supererogation

Voluntary works—besides, over and above God's commandments—which are called works of supererogation, cannot be taught without arrogancy and impiety. For by them men do declare that they do not only render unto God as much as they are bound to do, but that they do more for his sake than of bounden duty is required; whereas Christ saith plainly: When ye have done all that is commanded of you, say, We are unprofitable servants.

SCRIPTURAL BASIS: "Is it any pleasure to the Almighty, that thou art righteous? or is it gain to him, that thou makest thy ways perfect?" (Job 22:3.) "So likewise ye, when ye shall have done all those things which are commanded you, say, We are unprofitable servants: we have done that which was our duty to do." (Luke 17:10.)

The Roman Catholic Church has a teaching against which Article 11 is directed. It holds that there is an immense "treasury of merit," composed of the pious deeds of Christ and of the saints, and that this treasury can be made applicable to the benefit of others. In other words a modern Christian can draw upon the bank account of goodness stored up by others.

The Bible knows nothing of this. The "circle of *duty* takes in the entire ability of man, and therefore leaves no room for the works of supererogation." [7] We can never do enough good anyhow, and each man must stand on his own record and not on that of another.

Incidentally it may be said that out of this Romish doctrine of supererogation came the evil system of selling indulgences—a procedure which so shocked Martin Luther that he began the Reformation in protest against this and other abuses of the Roman Church.

[7] *Ibid.*

12. Of Sin After Justification

Not every sin willingly committed after justification is the sin against the Holy Spirit, and unpardonable. Wherefore, the grant of repentance is not to be denied to such as fall into sin after justification: after we have received the Holy Spirit, we may depart from grace given, and fall into sin, and, by the grace of God, rise again and amend our lives. And therefore they are to be condemned who say they can no more sin as long as they live here; or deny the place of forgiveness to such as truly repent.

SCRIPTURAL BASIS: "Return, ye backsliding children, and I will heal your backslidings." (Jer. 3:22.) "If any man sin, we have an advocate with the Father, Jesus Christ the righteous." (I John 2:1.) "If we confess our sins, he is faithful and just to forgive us our sins." (I John 1:9.) "Remember therefore from whence thou art fallen, and repent, and do the first works." (Rev. 2:5.)

Certain ancient church fathers held that when a person was forgiven and made a child of God, he was saved forever; but that if he should sin grievously again, he would by that act forfeit every chance to be saved. Article 12 says this is not so. It brushes aside the unreal belief that when a person is once saved, he cannot sin again. Unfortunately he can—as the lives of many have abundantly shown. Our Church, building solidly on experience, holds that just as we may "depart from grace given, and fall into sin," so we may by the same grace "rise again and amend our lives."

This is the well-known falling-from-grace doctrine of Methodism. It admits that even though once completely forgiven, a person can sin again; but asserts that such sin is not unpardonable. Just as one can fall, so one can rise. Isaac Watts wrote:

> And while the lamp holds out to burn,
> The vilest sinner may return.

Nowhere in the Bible can one find any warrant for denying the place of forgiveness to such as truly repent.

Article 12 also opens up the old question of the unpardonable sin. What is it? Many persons have worried greatly for fear they have sinned against the Holy Ghost. Our Methodist fathers, following sound doctrine, have always held that the unpardonable sin is not so much a certain act of willful transgression as it is a long, deliberate, defiance of the Spirit of grace. "The unpardonable state is *in the man,* not in the unwillingness of God to forgive." [8]

Those who worry as to whether they have sinned unpardonably need worry no more. For those who have really sinned unforgivably will never worry about it. They are already dead spiritually, and after a time even the very grace of God itself does not reach them. Therefore one who is deeply concerned as to whether or not he has committed the unpardonable sin may be sure that he has *not* committed it.

13. Of the Church

The visible Church of Christ is a congregation of faithful men in which the pure Word of God is preached, and the Sacraments duly administered according to Christ's ordinance, in all those things that of necessity are requisite to the same.

SCRIPTURAL BASIS: "Unto the church of God . . . , to them that are sanctified in Christ Jesus, called to the saints, with all that in every place call upon the name of Jesus Christ our Lord both theirs and ours." (I Cor. 1:2.) "And he gave some, apostles; and some, prophets; and some, evangelists; and some, pastors and teachers; for the perfecting of the saints, for the work of the ministry, for the edifying

[8] *Ibid.*

47

of the body of Christ." (Eph. 4:11-12.) "The church of God, which he hath purchased with his own blood." (Acts 20:28.)

This authoritative definition of the visible Church came to Methodism through the Lutheran and Reformed Church confessions. It makes no attempt to define the Church invisible, that holy and true fellowship whose membership is known to God alone. It speaks of the visible or earthly Church, which it calls first a "congregation." It is not a particular type of priesthood, nor of specially ordained men, but a fellowship of people imbued with Christian faith. This is the apostolic idea. This is the Church of the New Testament.

The true visible Church also hears the "pure Word of God" preached. That is to say, in every real church the gospel in its strength and power is always proclaimed. Likewise in every true church the Sacraments, which were ordained of Christ, are administered according to his direction.

On this definition we stand. Where there are congregations of faithful people, where the pure Word is preached and the Sacraments duly administered, there is the visible Church. Methodism delights to find true churches among people of all denominations. The faith of the people, the purity of the preached Word, and the due administration of the Sacraments —these things make and mark the Church on earth.

14. Of Purgatory

The Romish doctrine concerning purgatory, pardon, worshiping, and adoration, as well of images as of relics, and also invocation of saints, is a fond thing, vainly invented, and grounded upon no warrant of Scripture, but repugnant to the Word of God.

SCRIPTURAL BASIS: "Who can forgive sins but God only?" (Mark 2:7.) "Thou shalt not make unto thee any graven image." (Exod.

20:4.) "Thou shalt worship the Lord thy God, and him only shalt thou serve." (Matt. 4:10.)

This article is Protestantism's answer to erroneous teachings of the Roman Catholic Church. Purgatory, worshiping images and relics, the priest pronouncing pardon—such beliefs and practices are not found at all in the New Testament and indeed did not come into the Roman Catholic Church until the Middle Ages. There is not a scintilla of evidence in the Scriptures to support the idea of purgatory. The worship and adoration of images and relics, and the invoking of the saints through prayer, are hostile to the whole spirit of Protestantism. Protestantism does respect and venerate holy lives of the past and the present, but it yields worship only to God. "Thou shalt worship the Lord thy God, and him only."

As to pardon we do believe in that, but it is God's pardon, not man's. No priestly absolution can convey what God only can give, for "who can forgive sins but God only?" (Mark 2:7). Our Lord taught us to ask our heavenly Father for forgiveness when we need it—as, sadly enough, we often do. "Our Father, ... forgive us our trespasses."

15. Of Speaking in the Congregation in Such a Tongue as the People Understand

It is a thing plainly repugnant to the Word of God, and the custom of the primitive Church, to have public prayer in the Church, or to administer the Sacraments, in a tongue not understood by the people.

SCRIPTURAL BASIS: "He that speaketh in an unknown tongue speaketh not unto men, but unto God: for no man understandeth him. ... In the church I had rather speak five words with my understanding ... than ten thousand words in an unknown tongue." (I Cor. 14:2, 19.)

The Roman Catholic Church carries on its services and administers its sacraments in Latin. The Reformers, who wrote this particular article, cited the scripture given above against such a practice. They also called attention to the custom of the primitive Church in which people certainly did not preach or speak or pray in a language foreign to their life. Origen, an early church father, said in A.D. 202: "The Grecians pray to God in the Greek; the Romans in the Roman; everyone in his own tongue." Religion means nothing at all if it cannot be translated into the life and language and the hearts of people.

16. Of the Sacraments

Sacraments ordained of Christ are not only badges or tokens of Christian men's profession, but rather they are certain signs of grace, and God's good will toward us, by which he doth work invisibly in us, and doth not only quicken, but also strengthen and confirm, our faith in him.

There are two Sacraments ordained of Christ our Lord in the Gospel; that is to say, Baptism and the Supper of the Lord.

Those five commonly called sacraments, that is to say, confirmation, penance, orders, matrimony, and extreme unction, are not to be counted for Sacraments of the Gospel; being such as have partly grown out of the *corrupt* following of the apostles, and partly are states of life allowed in the Scriptures, but yet have not the like nature of Baptism and the Lord's Supper, because they have not any visible sign or ceremony ordained of God.

The Sacraments were not ordained of Christ to be gazed upon, or to be carried about; but that we should duly use them. And in such only as worthily receive the same they have a wholesome effect or operation; but they

**that receive them unworthily, purchase to themselves
condemnation, as St. Paul saith, I Cor. 11:29.**

SCRIPTURAL BASIS: Christ ordained but two true sacraments—baptism and the Lord's Supper. (See Matt. 26:26; 28:19; I Cor. 11:23.)
"Go ye therefore, and teach all nations, baptizing them in the name
of the Father, and of the Son, and of the Holy Ghost." (Matt. 28:
19.) "And as they were eating, Jesus took bread, and blessed it, and
brake it, and gave it to the disciples, and said, Take, eat; this is
my body." (Matt. 26:26.) "For I have received of the Lord that
which also I delivered unto you, That the Lord Jesus the same night
in which he was betrayed took bread: and when he had given thanks,
he brake it, and said, Take, eat: this is my body, which is broken
for you: this do in remembrance of me." (I Cor. 11:23, 24.)

As the next two articles will deal with each of the sacraments, a more complete explanation will be given there. The
present article declares what are true sacraments and how
these should be reverenced and received.

This particular article mentions other rites and ceremonies
which are taken as sacraments by the Roman Catholic Church.
Protestants agree that some of these sacred observances are
worthy of reverence and respect—for instance, confirmation
as well as the rite of ordination into the ministry of the
church, and the ceremony of marriage. These are sacred observances worthy to be hallowed by the good will and prayers
of Christian people. Yet, as Article 16 states, these rites are
not to be counted as equal to the two sacraments ordained by
Christ.

Two other rites called sacraments by the Church of Rome,
penance and extreme unction, are viewed with distaste by
Protestants. Penance, of course, we believe in as a Godly
penitence for sin; but it needs no priestly rite to make it
effective, and no human being can pronounce forgiveness.
Extreme unction, the anointing given by the priest to the dy-

ing, may be carried out earnestly and sincerely. However, neither penance nor extreme unction has any warrant in scripture, and they are not sacraments as we understand the term.

17. Of Baptism

Baptism is not only a sign of profession and mark of difference whereby Christians are distinguished from others that are not baptized; but it is also a sign of regeneration or the new birth. The baptism of young children is to be retained in the church.

SCRIPTURAL BASIS: "Arise, and be baptized, and wash away thy sins, calling on the name of the Lord." (Acts 22:16.) "Except a man be born of water and of the Spirit, he cannot enter into the kingdom of God." (John 3:5.) "He that believeth and is baptized shall be saved." (Mark 16:16.)

This article calls baptism a *sign* of profession and a *sign* of regeneration—not regeneration itself. To be sure, baptism is an institution of our Lord and so is to be kept and carried out as he commanded. But Protestantism has never put heavy emphasis upon the rite of baptism as having of itself any great value. It signifies something beyond itself. In Christian minds it symbolizes the receiving of the Holy Spirit, and all baptismal prayers uttered by the Church are to the effect that the one who is baptized shall also be baptized with the Holy Spirit.

Our Church holds that the sacrament of baptism ought to be administered to young children in the name of Christ. It is a token of their initiation into the gospel way and ought to be observed by Christian parents everywhere according to Christ's ordinance. (For further discussion of infant baptism see page 148.)

18. Of the Lord's Supper

The Supper of the Lord is not only a sign of the love that Christians ought to have among themselves one to another, but rather is a sacrament of our redemption by Christ's death; insomuch that, to such as rightly, worthily, and with faith receive the same, the bread which we break is a partaking of the body of Christ; and likewise the cup of blessing is a partaking of the blood of Christ.

Transubstantiation, or the change of the substance of bread and wine in the Supper of our Lord, cannot be proved by Holy Writ, but is repugnant to the plain words of Scripture, overthroweth the nature of a sacrament, and hath given occasion to many superstitions.

The body of Christ is given, taken, and eaten in the Supper, only after a heavenly and spiritual manner. And the means whereby the body of Christ is received and eaten in the Supper is faith.

The Sacrament of the Lord's Supper was not by Christ's ordinance reserved, carried about, lifted up, or worshiped.

SCRIPTURAL BASIS: "And he took bread, and gave thanks, and brake it, and gave unto them, saying, This is my body which is given for you: this do in remembrance of me. Likewise also the cup after supper, saying, This cup is the new testament in my blood, which is shed for you." (Luke 22:19-20.)

The greatest symbol of the Christian Church is the sacrament of the Lord's Supper. In this Christian people remember what the Lord did for them and pray that in turn they may give themselves as living sacrifices to his service.

In this sacrament the bread and wine—or the elements, as we commonly call them—signify the body and blood of our Lord Jesus Christ. They are received and eaten in a spiritual, that is, a heavenly, manner; and all the fathers and teachers of the Church have emphasized that the means whereby this is done is *faith*.

There is nothing automatic or mechanical about the Supper of the Lord. He who does not take it reverently and sincerely, or he whose heart is not open by faith, cannot receive its benefits. But when the Lord's Supper is genuinely and seriously entered into with a desire to walk more closely in his holy ways, then indeed it becomes a means of grace and "very full of comfort."

The Roman Catholic doctrine of transubstantiation (which holds that at the word of the priest the bread and wine are miraculously transformed into the actual body and blood of the Lord) is completely repudiated by this article. So also is rejected the idea that the sacrament itself, that is, the elements of the sacrament, have magic properties. The Church of Rome has public processions in which the Host (sacrament) is carried ostentatiously about for the adoration and worship of the people. It is what happens *within* the believer, not what happens without, that makes for the true sacrament.

19. Of Both Kinds

The cup of the Lord is not to be denied to the lay people; for both the parts of the Lord's Supper, by Christ's ordinance and commandment, ought to be administered to all Christians alike.

SCRIPTURAL BASIS: "He took the cup, and gave thanks, and gave it to them [the disciples], saying, Drink ye all of it." (Matt. 26: 27.) "For as often as ye [believers in common] eat this bread, and drink this cup, ye do shew the Lord's death till he come. . . . But let a man [the believer] examine himself, and so let him eat of that bread, and drink of that cup." (I Cor. 11:26, 28.)

Both the bread and wine were administered by our Lord to his apostles—as all accounts of the original Lord's Supper agree. They were to be given and partaken in remembrance of Christ until his coming again. So the command which we repeat at the Communion service is "Drink ye all of this"— that is, "All of you, drink." There was never any idea of keeping the cup from the lay people until a comparatively late date in the Roman Catholic Church. Then the Church of Rome, in support of its teaching of transubstantiation, affirmed that the cup need not be given since the "flesh contains the blood." The Roman Catholic Church thereafter ceased to pass the cup to its lay people.

Protestantism gloriously brushes aside all such unwarranted ideas. It insists that lay people and ministers are alike before God and so has restored the idea of a real fellowship or communion. In this neither priest nor minister stands in any way above the people. All together take the bread and wine in remembrance of their risen Lord.

20. Of the One Oblation of Christ, Finished upon the Cross

The offering of Christ, once made, is that perfect redemption, propitiation, and satisfaction for all the sins of the whole world, both original and actual; and there is none other satisfaction for sin but that alone. Wherefore the sacrifice of masses, in the which it is commonly said that the priest doth offer Christ for the quick and the dead, to have remission of pain or guilt, is a blasphemous fable and dangerous deceit.

SCRIPTURAL BASIS: "So Christ was once offered to bear the sins of many." (Heb. 9:28.) "Knowing that Christ being raised from the dead dieth no more. . . . For in that he died, he died unto sin once." (Rom. 6:9, 10.) "Neither is there salvation in any other: for there is none other name under heaven given among men, whereby we must be saved." (Acts 4:12.) "There remaineth no more sacrifice for sins." (Heb. 10:26.) "After he had offered one sacrifice for sins for ever, [he] sat down on the right hand of God: . . . For by one offering he hath perfected for ever them that are sanctified." (Heb. 10:12, 14.)

This scriptural, Christian view of the sacrifice of Christ is a powerful expression of Protestant faith. It stands as an everlasting denial of the Roman idea that the sacrifice of Christ can be repeated every time the priest says a Mass. Methodism, with all Protestantism, holds that what Christ did on Calvary was done once and for all, that his sacrifice was a "full, perfect, and sufficient sacrifice, oblation, and satisfaction for the sins of the whole world." What is done at the Supper of the Lord is in "memory of his precious death until his coming again." No one can ever repeat Christ's sacrifice.

The Roman Catholic doctrine holds that in the Mass the priest has the miraculous power to cause the bread and wine to become the actual body of Christ again, and then he offers Christ's body (and so "says a mass") for some particular cause or sin. In other words Calvary is supposed to take place again each time the Mass is celebrated.

Our English reformer ancestors repudiated this idea of the Mass so completely and so plainly that they used the bluntest of blunt English to describe it: "a blasphemous fable and a dangerous deceit."

21. Of the Marriage of Ministers

The ministers of Christ are not commanded by God's law either to vow the estate of single life, or to abstain from marriage; therefore it is lawful for them, as for all other Christians, to marry at their own discretion, as they shall judge the same to serve best to godliness.

SCRIPTURAL BASIS: The apostle Peter was a married man. "When Jesus was come into Peter's house, he saw his wife's mother laid, and sick of a fever." (Matt. 8:14.) Philip, the evangelist, had "four daughters, virgins, which did prophesy." (Acts 21:9.) Paul says: "A bishop then must be blameless, the husband of one wife" (I Tim. 3:2.) "Let the deacons be the husband of one wife." (I Tim. 3:12.) "Have we not power to lead about . . . a wife, as well as other apostles?" (I Cor. 9:5.)

Here is another anti-Romish Article, for the Church of Rome has commanded its priests never to marry. Each one of them, therefore, gives up any possibility of a home and family. This procedure has no warrant in scripture. Indeed, Peter, who is claimed by the Roman Church to have been the first pope, was a married man; and so were many of the apostles and Christian bishops until a rather late date. Then Rome, keeping its priests cut off from everything on earth but its own iron discipline, forbade them to marry.

Protestantism follows the practice of the early Church. Ministers may marry or refrain from marrying according to their own discretion.

22. Of the Rites and Ceremonies of Churches

It is not necessary that rites and ceremonies should in all places be the same, or exactly alike; for they have been always different, and may be changed according to the diversity of countries, times, and men's manners, so that nothing be ordained against God's Word. Whosoever, through his private judgment, willingly and purposely doth openly break the rites and ceremonies of the church to which he belongeth, which are not repugnant to the Word of God, and are ordained and approved by common authority, ought to be rebuked openly (that others may fear to do the like), as one that offendeth

against the common order of the church, and woundeth the consciences of weak brethren.

Every particular church may ordain, change, or abolish rites and ceremonies, so that all things may be done to edification.

SCRIPTURAL BASIS: "As free, and not using your liberty for a cloak of maliciousness, but as the servants of God." (I Pet. 2:16.) "Let every man be fully persuaded in his own mind." (Rom. 14:5.) "Let all things be done unto edifying." (I Cor. 14:26.)

The breadth and freedom of the Christian faith is made clear in Article 22. This recognizes frankly that in different countries and places Christians will have different ways of worship. Such divergence is to be approved. Every church, therefore, is allowed to have the right to change its rites and ceremonies as it pleases so long as "all things [are] done to edification"—in other words so long as all things are agreeable to true Christian faith and its expression.

Let it be noted that the privilege of ordering and arranging rites and ceremonies belongs to a *church*, not to an *individual*. For the article goes on to say that "whosoever, *through his private judgment,* willingly and purposely doth openly break the rites and ceremonies of the church to which he belongeth" ought to be rebuked. Thus the church itself may establish and change its own rites and ceremonies, but no private individual is allowed to do so. This provision of the article is sometimes overlooked.

23. Of the Rulers of the United States of America

The President, the Congress, the general assemblies, the governors, and the councils of state *as the delegates of the people,* are the rulers of the United States of America, according to the division of power made to them by the Constitution of the United States and by

the constitutions of their respective states. And the said states are a sovereign and independent nation, and ought not to be subject to any foreign jurisdiction.

SCRIPTURAL BASIS: "Render therefore unto Caesar the things which are Caesar's; and unto God the things that are God's." (Matt. 22: 21.) "Let every soul be subject unto the higher powers. For there is no power but of God: the powers that be are ordained of God. . . . For rulers are not a terror to good works, but to the evil. . . . For he is the minister of God to thee for good." (Rom. 13:1, 3, 4.)

When John Wesley sent over twenty-four Articles of Religion to American Methodism, he selected them one by one from the Thirty-nine Articles of the Church of England. Now among the Thirty-nine Articles is one which certifies to the faith of the Church of England in the supremacy of the king. Wesley, who knew that America had won its liberty from the British king, therefore omitted this article entirely. But the Methodist fathers in organizing the Methodist Episcopal Church at the Christmas Conference felt that there ought to be in the faith of the new church some reference to the rulers of the land. So they wrote the present Article 23, declaring that the President, the Congress, and the various authorities named are the "rulers of the United States." They also backed up the Declaration of Independence—only eight years old at that time—by declaring the United States to be sovereign and independent. Church and state are separate in America, but The Methodist Church *makes the independence of the United States part of its fundamental faith.*

In Methodist churches established in such nations as Japan, Brazil, Mexico, and so on, this article has been changed or adapted so as to affirm recognition of those who are the established authorities in each particular land.

24. Of Christian Men's Goods

The riches and goods of Christians are not common, as touching the right, title, and possession of the same, as some do falsely boast. Notwithstanding, every man ought, of such things as he possesseth, liberally to give alms to the poor, according to his ability.

SCRIPTURAL BASIS: The commandment "Thou shalt not steal" (Exod. 20:15) implies ownership of property. "Give to him that asketh thee, and from him that would borrow of thee turn not thou away." (Matt. 5:42.) Giving and lending also necessarily imply the personal ownership of property. "But whoso hath this world's good, and seeth his brother have need, and shutteth up his bowels of compassion from him, how dwelleth the love of God in him?" (I John 3:17.)

Article 24, as it deals with economics, is of great import today. It was written in opposition to the teaching advanced by pious groups in Europe just after the Reformation to the effect that Christian people had no inherent right to be the owners of private property. To be a Christian, they said, one must divide all that he has with all other people. This, of course, is communism, though the system that went by that name in earlier times was different in its ideals from modern dictator-dominated communism.

It is quite true that the early Christians did for a time have "all things [in] common," as the book of Acts tells us (4:32). But this plan did not work with as saintly a group as the early Christians, and it will not work any better today. A communistic society can never operate unless its will is enforced by a ruthless police power, which is the very breath of life to such a system.

Our Christian forebears in England considered this article necessary as an affirmation that each Christian *does* have a right to his own possessions. Our church teaches that the title to one's private property is inherent in the individual. However, this Article of Religion guards against a rapacious capitalism by affirming that every man out of his (private) possessions must give to the poor according to his ability—meaning that each Christian must share with others. Neither communism nor a selfish possessiveness is therefore the Christian answer, but *stewardship,* in which each man truly and rightfully owns his own goods and values, but holds them *in trust for God and his fellow man.* In other words our goods are ours to make them God's.

25. Of a Christian Man's Oath

As we confess that vain and rash swearing is forbidden Christian men by our Lord Jesus Christ and James his apostle; so we judge that the Christian religion doth not prohibit, but that a man may swear when the magistrate requireth, in a cause of faith and charity, so it be done according to the prophet's teaching, in justice, judgment, and truth.

SCRIPTURAL BASIS: "And thou shalt swear, The Lord liveth, in truth, in judgment, and in righteousness." (Jer. 4:2.) "Men verily swear by the greater: and an oath for confirmation is to them an end of all strife." (Heb. 6:16.) "And Jonathan caused David to swear again." (I Sam. 20:17.) "I call God for a record upon my soul." (II Cor. 1:23.)

The Quakers and other sects, at the time these articles were written, did not believe that it was right to swear an oath before a magistrate. They took our Lord's injunction "Swear not at all" to be a direct command against affirming anything at law. Our church holds that rash and vain swearing is forbidden, of course, by the New Testament; but we "judge," as the fathers here put it, that the Christian religion does not keep a man from taking a solemn oath when a magistrate requireth it "in a cause of faith and charity."

A Christian's oath, however, ought to be given reverently in justice, in judgment, and in truth. Lightness or levity in making affirmation or in stating what one cannot know to be true—all this is forbidden not only by the Word of God but by the common sense of the Christian brotherhood.

CHAPTER THREE

Prominent Doctrines

METHODISM has emphasized certain Christian doctrines so heavily that they have come to be regarded by some as distinctively Methodist. These are:

REGENERATION—The new birth, through which one becomes a child of God.

THE WITNESS OF THE SPIRIT—The certification which each Christian may have that he is a child of God.

THE POSSIBILITY OF FINAL PERFECTION—The teaching that it is possible and intended that everyone shall live a sinless life and be "made perfect in love" in this life.

Other doctrines also greatly stressed have been:

REPENTANCE—A godly sorrow for sin coupled with a will to sin no more. Repentance of course must precede any complete turning to God.

UNIVERSAL REDEMPTION—That Christ died for all, not simply a chosen number.

JUSTIFICATION BY FAITH—The great affirmation of the Protestant Reformation. This has been, and is, a Methodist doctrine as it is for all who rightly walk in the Christian way. Its meaning has been explained under Article 9, page 42.

Regeneration

THE NEW BIRTH, as Christians have long called it, is that act of God through which one is brought into his kingdom and experiences a change of heart. In the Scripture this experience is described as being "born again."

SCRIPTURAL BASIS: "Jesus . . . said . . . , Verily, I say unto thee, Except a man be born again, he cannot see the kingdom of God." (John 3:3.) "Being born again, not of corruptible seed, but of incorruptible, by the word of God, which liveth and abideth forever." (I Pet. 1:23.) "If any man be in Christ, he is a new creature." (II Cor. 5:17.) . . . "Which were born, not of blood, nor of the will of the flesh, nor of the will of man, but of God." (John 1:13.) "That ye put on the new man, which after God is created in righteousness and true holiness." (Eph. 4:24.)

There is a very real sense in which this doctrine, or rather the thing it affirms, is the foundation of everything for a Christian. For unless and until a person becomes a Christian, how can he live a Christian life? How can he be heir to all Christian beliefs and promises? It has been the cardinal fallacy of the Church and ministry through the ages to treat as Christians those who in reality are not Christians, and to expect from such persons all Christian graces and attainments when they had never become Christian in the first place. "Ye must be born again" is the injunction that underlies every other Christian command.

But this becoming a Christian is not something one does for himself but something that God does for him. Each person, to be sure, must co-operate by repenting of his past sins and sincerely intend to lead a new life and sin no more. He must believe that God can and will save him—so much each one must do if he would find God, or rather, have God find him.

But the giving of a new spiritual life, the actual regenerative act, is by the power of God and God alone. Souls are born anew not "of the will of the flesh, nor of the will of man, but of God," as John says (1:13). The Church itself lacks regenerative power. It can receive a person into its fellowship by an outward act of reception; it can baptize one and pray that "he may be numbered with God's people here, and with his saints in glory everlasting"; it can put his name on its roll and make him feel at home—but the actual creative work, the dynamic work, the regenerative work of quickening one who has been "dead in trespasses and sin"—that belongs to God.

"How can this be?" Nicodemus asked Jesus when Jesus told him that man had need to be born again.

"The wind blows where it wills," replied the Master, "and you hear the sound of it, but you do not know whence it comes or whither it goes; so it is with every one who is born of the Spirit." (John 3:8 R.S.V.)

Life and scripture both join here to give undeniable testimony. The New Testament is filled with the accounts of those who were taken by God to become his children. So is the history of the Church, past and present. All revivals of religion have emphasized the new birth. No ceremony nor churchly process nor official pronouncement can ever be substituted for it.

A caution, however, can here be given. Being regenerate and born again is one thing; *knowing exactly when* one has been born again is something else. Many sincere Christians have not been able to tell when they became Christians. But they know they *are*.

It is at this point that certain earnest evangelists of early days, and some today, are inclined to be dogmatic. "If you don't know when you were saved, you are not saved," was the way these men put it. This is not sound reasoning. A clear thinker once countered this statement by saying, "If you don't remember when you were born, you never have been born at all"—which is ridiculous of course, as he meant it to be.

The truth is, human temperament seems to have something to do with the type of conversion experienced—that is, with one's regeneration. Persons who are of strong, decisive make-up usually have a cataclysmic conversion—that is, a soul-shaking one—if they are converted at all. Like the apostle Paul, who was of that type, they get knocked down, as it were, by the roadside and have their lives suddenly reversed. Of course such persons never forget the day nor hour. Augustine and John Wesley were other leaders of the Church who could point to a definite soul-shaking experience. So can many preachers and sincere laymen.

But there are quieter, more even-tempered persons, like Tertullian, the Christian thinker, who said that he "had a mind naturally religious" from his youth up. Such people usually grow in grace from childhood, and God's regenerative work, like the growing of the grass or the opening of the flowers in the spring, is almost imperceptible in degree, though glorious in its full fruition.

The important thing is for each person, of whatever type, to *know* that he has "passed from death unto life" and is a child of God. Whether by crisis or "lysis," as a doctor of medicine once put it; by a sudden explosive change or by a gradual one, just so that we have become God's children—that is the essential thing.

The Witness of the Spirit

SCRIPTURAL BASIS: "The Spirit itself beareth witness with our spirit, that we are the children of God." (Rom. 8:16.) "He that believeth on the Son of God hath the witness in himself." (I John 5:10.) "Because ye are sons, God hath sent forth the Spirit of his Son into your hearts, crying, Abba, Father." (Gal. 4:6.) "The love of God is shed abroad in our hearts by the Holy Ghost."

(Rom. 5:5.) "The fruit of the Spirit is love, joy, peace, longsuffering, gentleness, goodness, faith, meekness, temperance." (Gal. 5: 22-23.)

Here is another Christian truth of great import—the WITNESS OF THE SPIRIT. It means that the Holy Spirit in the heart of a believer can and does give him a firsthand assurance that he is a child of God. Paul stated this truth in his never-to-be forgotten words "The Spirit itself beareth witness with our spirit, that we are the children of God." The apostle knew, as he wrote this passage, that all other Christians would understand exactly what he meant.

Methodists, with other Christians, rejoice, as did the apostle, in the knowledge that God does certify unmistakably to each believer when his salvation is sure. But because this idea has sometimes been considered presumptuous or misguided, or may rise from inward feelings which have no basis in outward fact, it has been heavily attacked by many Christian thinkers. John Wesley himself, while he preached and taught the truth of the divine witness, was very careful to say exactly what he meant by it.

"By the testimony of the Spirit," he wrote, "I mean, an inward impression on the soul, whereby the Spirit of God immediately and directly witnesses to my spirit, that I am a child of God; that Jesus Christ hath loved me, and given Himself for me; that all my sins are blotted out, and I, even I, am reconciled to God."

The real question here is: Can a man truly *know* that he is a child of God? Not can a man *hope* so or *think* so. Can he *know?* Methodism with all the force of personal testimony has put together Bible doctrine and its own experience to say that one certainly can. Let us look at this a bit more.

The witness of the Spirit does not discount the fact that there are many things a Christian can learn for himself by study of the Bible and by living the Christian life. For instance, a person knows when he is doing right, when he is following the laws of God, when he has a good conscience, when with mind and strength and heart and soul he is endeavoring to follow God's holy will and commandment. Common sense tells one whether he is or is not in line with the purposes of God.

But what the witness of the Spirit means is that above and beyond the testimony of one's own conscience something else comes in—something tremendous—even the "testimony of God's Spirit, which is superadded to and conjoined" to one's own, Wesley put it.

It is at this point that a crass world begins to demur. "It is all right to *hope* and *reason* that you are a child of God," it is said, "but to be *sure* of it and to say that God makes you sure, that is to claim more than one has a right to claim."

It certainly is claiming a great deal, but those who have felt the inner witness have never doubted. They admit that there may be enthusiasts who imagine they have received blessings which perhaps they have not received, that there may be erratic persons who make all sorts of claims which are not "according to knowledge." Wesley himself wrote, "How many have mistaken the voice of their own imagination for this 'witness of the Spirit of God,' and thence idly presumed, they were the children of God, while they were doing the works of the devil? These are truly and properly enthusiasts." But the same Wesley went on to say the "testimony of the Spirit [is] an inward impression on the soul, whereby the Spirit of God immediately and directly witnesses to my spirit, that I am a child of God"—the quotation of Wesley which has just been cited on the previous page.

Wesley admits, however (after all his explanation), that "he who hath that witness in himself, cannot explain it to one who hath it not." He even adds: "Nor indeed is it to be expected that he should." But it can be preached, it can be taught, it can be claimed by those who have felt it, and it can be received, and we dare say it is, by those who sincerely and earnestly pray God for it. "If ye then, being evil, know how to give good gifts unto your children: how much more shall your heavenly Father give the Holy Spirit to them that ask him?" (Luke 11:13.)

Perhaps not all Christians have received the witness of the Spirit; perhaps God has not chosen to give it to each and every one—for the divine witness is not something we can wrest from heaven by force, nor take from God by pressing certain spiritual buttons. It is a priceless divine gift, albeit one that has been promised to those who diligently seek for it.

A man once joined a fraternal order in which after an initiation the new member was always presented with a badge of his fellowship. But when the secretary of the lodge went to get the badge, he was embarrassed to find that the supply had become exhausted. "I am sorry," he said to the newly initiated brother; "we let our supply run out. But we will write right away and get some more. Don't forget to claim yours in a few days, for *you have got it coming to you.*"

A weak illustration perhaps, but the sincere Christian can feel with due reverence that he has "coming to him" the Gift of the Spirit. Let him seek until he finds, knock and keep on knocking until the gift is given, and then he with the Christians of the ages will *know*. Seek it, brother, seek it. And when you find it, you will need no book to tell you what we are talking about.

Universal Redemption

SCRIPTURAL BASIS: "That he by the grace of God should taste death for every man." (Heb. 2:9.) "He is the propitiation for our sins: and not for ours only, but also for the sins of the whole world." (I John 2:2.) "The grace of God that bringeth salvation hath appeared to all men." (Tit. 2:11.) "God so loved the world, that he gave his only begotten Son, that whosoever believeth in him should not perish, but have everlasting life." (John 3:16.) "God our Saviour . . . will have all men to be saved." (I Tim. 2:3-4.)

UNIVERSAL REDEMPTION was the teaching that Methodism proclaimed eagerly and gladly in its formative years when it was up against the Calvinistic doctrine that Christ had died for the elect only, or for those only who were foreordained to be saved. Calvinism, always strong on logic, said that since only the elect were saved, the death of Christ and the redemption he brought was for them and them only—for who else got it?

Brushing this reasoning away as words which darken counsel, Methodists took up the resounding slogan "Universal Redemption" as a sort of war cry. Christ died for every man, not a select group—this was the affirmation that caught the ear of the multitudes who thronged the commons of England and packed the log chapels of the American frontier to hear the Methodists preach. Charles Wesley sang:

> O for a trumpet voice,
>   On all the world to call!
> To bid their hearts rejoice
>   In him who died for all!
> For all my Lord was crucified;
> For all, for all my Saviour died.

Hope and promise, not for a few, but for everyone, rang out in such hymns and in such preaching.

Universal redemption is not preached so often today, simply because it is not doubted now as it once was. The battle against that aspect of ironclad predestination has been completely won. Therefore, while we hold this doctrine as solidly as ever, we do not affirm it constantly as once we did because we do not need to. But if it were to be challenged again, we would renew the battle as energetically as ever.

Falling from Grace

In this brief outline of special Methodist beliefs a word more should be said about falling from grace. The "possibility of final apostasy" is the technical name for the unlovely fact that even the best of Christians may lose what they have.

It is surprising that falling from grace, which is at best a negative situation, should have been held up as such a positive doctrine of Methodism. That is, it would be surprising if falling from grace were not so palpably true in real life. In my treatment of the Articles of Religion I mentioned those unrealistic persons who believe that "once in grace, always in grace"—that when Christ saves a man, the man always afterward stays saved. Would that he might! Methodists with all Christians would rejoice to believe that no man who has ever come to Christ can ever fall away. But alas for the weakness of human nature and the power of sin! "Watch ye and pray, lest ye enter into temptation," was the Lord's constant injunction to his own. "Lead us not into temptation, but deliver us from evil."

Instance after instance both in scripture and in life have occurred where those who have once tasted of God's salvation have later grown cold and fallen away. Even Paul was afraid "lest that by any means, when I have preached to others, I myself should be a castaway." Man can fall, we must admit; but man can rise again. Methodism does not

71

blink the facts here but with all Christians hopes all things, at the same time singing her great war song:

> My soul, be on thy guard;
>   Ten thousand foes arise;
> The hosts of sin are pressing hard,
>   To draw thee from the skies.
>
> .   .   .   .
>
> Ne'er think the victory won,
>   Nor lay thine armor down;
> The work of faith will not be done,
>   'Till thou obtain the crown.

Christian Perfection

Over against this negative and unlovely truth Methodism teaches what is called in technical language the "possibility of final perfection," or CHRISTIAN PERFECTION, as it is usually called.

This was the cardinal doctrine and daily pursuit of early Methodism—the ceaseless, unremitting endeavor to live a sinless life. Is it possible to live such a life when "all have sinned, and come short of the glory of God?" Methodists have always maintained not only that it is possible but that it is necessary to "follow . . . holiness, without which no man shall see the Lord" (Heb. 12:14); that God's commands are given to be obeyed, else they would not be given at all; and that God would but mock us had he given us commandments which he knew we could not possibly keep.

John Wesley taught that it was possible for a person to live every day in such a manner as to be blameless before God and man. He held that it was possible for one to be made "perfect in love" while he yet lived, and asked every preacher who joined the Methodist Conference to answer this question:

"Do you expect to be made perfect in love in this life?" That question is still asked of every preacher before he joins one of our Methodist conferences today. What exactly does it mean?

It does not mean that people should expect to be mentally or physically perfect while they live or that they can ever reach a state spiritually where there is no possibility of falling into sin. "Perfection," as W. E. Sangster of London once expressed it, "is an unfortunate term." It has about it an idea of something that is finished and fixed. That is not what the Christian means by this idea. He means that if we can live one day without sin, we can live two; if two, then many— why not all? So there can be a growing in grace and a drawing closer and closer to God each day until the time arrives when one literally becomes what God would have him be— and is not that a perfect man?

Wesley never claimed for himself that he had been "made perfect in [Christian] love," and some who have claimed it have been most clearly mistaken about themselves. But if God can by one creative act cause souls to be born into his kingdom, may not his grace, having daily sway in his people's lives, eventually fit them for living ever at home with him in the fullness and richness of his kingdom? Whether this comes by a single creative touch while one lives, or in the life everlasting, is in God's hands.

At any rate the doctrine of Christian perfection has been the one specific doctrinal contribution which Methodism has made to the Church universal. John Wesley called it the "peculiar doctrine committed to our trust." In all else we have been, as we should be, glad and energetic followers in the main stream of Christian belief. But in this one doctrine we stand by ourselves and utter a teaching that reaches up fearlessly and touches the very Scepter of God. Nerved by the tremendous, "Be ye holy; for I am holy," and "Be ye therefore perfect, even as your Father which is in heaven is perfect," we are to hope for ourselves and for others that we shall be made perfect in love in this life. And perhaps here again, as is our faith, so shall it be.

Evangelism and the Evangelistic Spirit

Closely connected with the doctrinal beliefs of Methodism has been its aggressive way of presenting them. This means evangelism and reaching the unreached. So energetically was the gospel pressed upon all by our Methodist forebears that Methodism came to be regarded as primarily an evangelistic movement—which it largely is. Always the evangelizing principle has been at the heart of it. We have not been content to see our own homes and families at peace in God's kingdom; we have wished for other families and other souls and have been greatly successful in bringing them in.

Methods of evangelizing vary; but the gospel is carried forward today, as in the past, primarily by the voice of man communicating the truths of God to other men. The pulpit through its preachers and teachers has led the way; but sincere laymen and women of the church, as they have spoken to other men and women, have played, and continue to play, a very great part.

There are two methods of evangelizing which the church has used with success. First and perhaps most effective, especially during Methodism's formative years, was *revival preaching*. The other method has been indicated above—that of personal approach by person to person. This last is often carried on today as *visitation evangelism*. Both methods hold great promise; both have had large results.

Evangelistic services and preaching missions have been wonderfully used by Methodism to express and implement its evangelistic zeal. Revivals, as such services were formerly called because of their announced intent, were really concentrated, intensive efforts to spread the gospel by setting apart periods for preaching to church people, and for calling sinners and "outsiders" to change their lives. Such periods have been of inestimable benefit.

Revival and evangelistic services are marked by:

1. Preaching which emphasizes and hammers away upon the absolute fundamentals of Christian life and duty—sin and its consequences, Christ as Saviour, Redeemer, and Lord of all life.

2. Direct pleas to lukewarm and indifferent church members to recapture the lost radiancy of faith and an even more direct plea to those afar from God to come to him and find life sweet and purposeful.

Such services have a certain cumulative effect. One sermon follows another; each plea intensifies those that have gone before. The net result is the stirring up of the church to greater activity and zeal, and the conversion of sinners through the work of reclaiming grace.

Every local church needs a period once a year when people are summoned to sit under strong gospel preaching; when they are urged to bring outsiders with them and to give, when opportunity allows, a sincere statement of what Christ means to them. Our church believes that it has the right to expect each professing Christian to take his place, when called upon to do so, in the firing line for God. Church-school teachers especially have a great opportunity here.

Visitation evangelism does not necessarily depend on periods of revival preaching for its effective work, though intensive preaching and the personal work of devoted Christian visitors go together and support each other. The visitation method has the advantage of reaching those who would never think of going within the walls of a church. It also gives an opportunity to laymen to reach the unreached by private personal appeal. Many a lay person, often to his own surprise, has proved to be unusually talented and successful as a visitation evangelist. Indeed visitation evangelism is largely a lay movement in present-day Methodism. The pastor gives inspiration and direction in all well-organized plans, but the laymen are the evangelizers—as was true in the days of the apostles.

In all evangelizing two things are needed:

First, a sure knowledge on the part of the one who carries the message of the things of which he speaks. He must get over to other men not something he has read in a book nor heard from a pulpit, but something he has experienced in life. Of course he has read the gospel story and heard gospel preaching and knows what others have said. But beyond all else there is the tremendous affirmation "I know," which is the strength of anyone who would help another find his way to God.

Second, the true evangelist must have an earnest desire that others will know and experience God's grace also. He is anxious to tell his message and see others converted. This used to be called a "concern for souls." It is always powerful within those who are conscious that God has done something in their own lives.

Evangelistic efforts arranged by some mechanical program of preaching or visitation, which has not at its heart both personal knowledge and sincere desire, will always fall far short of what is intended.

The Methodist Church intends today as in the past to continue its evangelistic efforts. To be sure, new techniques may be called for; but there is no substitute for presenting the word of God to man boldly, strongly, and pleadingly. It is a solemn fact that in those sections of the country where we have ceased to hold preaching missions and revivals with anything like regularity, our church has settled down simply to hold the ground we have. Sometimes we lose even that. On the contrary, where revivals are held continually and where evangelism is written large in the spirit of each local church, there is a growing and an increasing and a gathering in of people as a harvest unto God.

A church without revivals and conference areas where the revival spirit has died away are like troops doing cantonment duty—sitting down to routine garrison occupation. Where the gospel is preached and where sinners are called to repentance, where personal workers go out, and where men and women really are brought back from death unto life, there the church becomes glorious in its spiritual militancy. "Are we going to settle down and be simply an army of occupation?" an aggressive Methodist layman once challenged his fellows in the midst of an evangelistic campaign. "Or are we going to lead a cavalry charge?"

Other great denominations have copied Methodism in its methods of evangelism; and when they have, they have benefited amazingly. It will be tragic if we who have been great revivalists and evangelists shall forget our former ways. With all the crudeness and blatancy which have been displayed by certain evangelists, with all the crass, brassy showmanship which has been used, with all the pillorying of peoples' inmost feelings as they have been held up to public view, the revivalist and the evangelist can claim genuine converts by the thousands. It is true that many fall away after the heightened emotion of the revival period passes, but it is also true that many remain who have been turned from evil unto righteousness and who live ever after as examples that God's power can make bad people good.

"Evangelize or die" is the message that two thousand years of Christian history writes indelibly over the altar of every church.

CHAPTER FOUR

Discipline

DOCTRINE has to do with what one believes, discipline with what one does. Every Christian must follow certain principles of good conduct just as surely as he must hold to principles of true belief.

As was stated on an earlier page, the very name "Methodist" was given to the little group led by John Wesley because they were so methodical in the way they did things. It was their conviction that a good life ought to be made to count for God by what it does as well as by what it believes. So "discipline" has been a big word in Methodism. In the very beginning a series of rules was laid down by Wesley in order to teach his people how they might profitably use their time.

Wesley's rules are known as the GENERAL RULES. They are published in every issue of our book of *Discipline*; they are fixed in the written constitution of The Methodist Church (and not one of them can be changed except by amending the constitution—a long, difficult, and unlikely process). While our interpretation of these rules is somewhat different from that of our fathers, they are still the official rules of our Church; and they have always provided a systematic guide for Christian conduct.

Wesley drew up the General Rules in 1739 at the request of certain members of the Methodist societies. They asked him to give them a definite plan for Christian living. He did so, and from that day to this the General Rules have been at the heart of the Methodist movement.

The General Rules were not intended to be a complete system of Christian ethics. They presuppose that every Christian already knows right and wrong when it comes to great matters of Christian morality. Wesley gave no rule against murder or theft or adultery because he did not need to. Methodists, with all other Christians, are expected to live in line with God's Word at all times. What the General Rules do is emphasize and pinpoint Christian morality at stressful places in a methodical, practical, biblical way.

It may be worth noting that while our Methodist doctrine is quite broad, Methodist discipline has been thought by many to be extremely narrow. Especially in early days Methodists were considered "narrow" because of their strict manner of life. Even within the church itself there have been those who have complained from time to time over certain strict interpretations of the General Rules. But life and experience provided the final test, and no present-day Methodist need be ashamed of the result in character that came by obeying these time-honored rules.

The General Rules fall into three divisions. The first division may be called the *negative* rules. These represent those actions and those attitudes which a Christian must not take. Wesley explained as an introduction to this section that every Christian must first of all avoid evil of every kind, especially "that which is most generally practiced." Then he proceeded to tell the various things which represent the doing of positive evil.

The second division of the General Rules is *positive*. Christians must do all the good they can. Wesley here lists many Christian acts and procedures which are to be followed.

The third division enjoins *attendance upon all the ordinances* of God, such as public worship, Holy Communion, prayer (both at home and in public), Bible reading, and fasting.

Let us now examine the General Rules and their present-day application.

The Negative Rules

RULE ONE

[Against] the taking of the name of God in vain

SCRIPTIURAL BASIS: "Thou shalt not take the name of the Lord thy God in vain; for the Lord will not hold him guiltless that taketh his name in vain." (Exod. 20:7.)

This supports the Third Commandment. Cursing, swearing, and railing against God on the part of profane men has always been discountenanced among Christians everywhere. Modern church people sometimes have become careless in the way they use expletives and current explosive terms. Psychologically such expletives furnish something of relief, so the psychiatrists tell us; and within their degree harmless expressions of vehemence do no ill. But the name of God should not be brought into common conversation except in a most reverent way. "Thou shalt not take the name of the Lord thy God in vain" must be written anew today.

RULE TWO

[Against] the profaning the day of the Lord, either by doing ordinary work therein, or by buying or selling

SCRIPTURAL BASIS: The essential moral import of the Fourth Commandment has always been reflected in Christianity. "Remember the sabbath day, to keep it holy." (Exod. 20:8.)

Let it be noted that Wesley referred to Sunday as the "day of the Lord," not the "Sabbath." Puritanical legalism which would transfer to the Christian Sunday all the heavy burdens of the Jewish dispensation need not burden or weigh us down today. Nevertheless there is a sense in which the Lord's Day has been hallowed eternally by the resurrection of Christ and is to be kept in his name and for his glory and for the life and well-being of his Church. Whatever theories may be held regarding Sunday, the Christian Church and the Christian Sunday stand together; injure one and you injure the other.

A discerning writer some years ago said that if he were given control of American life, he would first of all restore the old-fashioned Sunday. "For," said he, "the old-fashioned Sunday was the best remedy ever devised to restore peace and sobriety to a jittery world."

In our time Sunday has come to be a day of recreation and within reason is one in which family life and home life can be developed and enjoyed in a quiet, Christian way.

Let it be admitted that of necessity there are some businesses which must be carried out on Sunday as well as on other days. But let us remember Sunday to keep it holy, not because of crystallized legality, but because of the richness and grace made possible by the day of our Lord.

Buying and selling on Sunday are specifically forbidden by this rule, and forbidden, too, by the deeper conscience of Christian men and women. Sunday should refit us for the six days in which we must labor. To do that, it must be a day especially dedicated to the worship and the remembrance of Almighty God.

RULE THREE

[Against] drunkenness, buying or selling spirituous

liquors, or drinking them, unless in cases of extreme necessity

SCRIPTURAL BASIS: The wisdom literature of the Bible condemns strong drink. "Be not among winebibbers; . . . for the drunkard and the glutton shall come to poverty." (Prov. 23:20-21.) "Wine is a mocker, strong drink is raging. . . . At the last it biteth like a serpent, and stingeth like an adder." (Prov. 20:1; 23:32.) The New Testament puts drinking in the whole context of the Christian life, where it sees it as evil. "Let us walk honestly, . . . not in rioting and drunkenness. . . . But put ye on the Lord Jesus Christ." (Rom. 13: 13-14.) "We are not of the night. . . . Therefore . . . let us watch and be sober." (I Thess. 5:5-6.) "Nor thieves, . . . nor drunkards, . . . shall inherit the kingdom of God." (I Cor. 6:10.)

From the very beginning our people have been a temperate people and have been opposed with all their hearts and souls to the buying and selling of intoxicating liquor. To be sure, in this rule Wesley made a distinction between spirituous liquors and presumably those which had been brewed. But the modern Methodist decisively rejects any distinction of this sort. The milder liquors lead on to the stronger ones, and there is something about the earnest Christian life which reacts violently against any kind of intoxicating drink. All theories go down before the terrific fact that every day lives are being wasted and ruined by strong drink. Let it not be tolerated by us! We cannot be at all lax here.

RULE FOUR

[Against] slaveholding; buying or selling slaves

In Wesley's time slaveholding was a burning moral issue, as it later became in the United States. Because today the judgment of both God and man condemns slavery everywhere, this rule is now only of historic interest.

RULE FIVE

[Against] fighting, quarreling, brawling, brother

going to law with brother; returning evil for evil, or railing for railing; the using of many words in buying or selling

SCRIPTURAL BASIS: "From whence come wars and fightings among you?—come they not hence, even of your lusts that war in your members?" (Jas. 4:1). "Now the works of the flesh are manifest which are these; . . . hatred, variance, emulations, wrath, strife, seditions, heresies." (Gal. 5:19, 20.) "Dare any of you, having a matter against another, go to law before the unjust, and not before the saints? Do ye not know that the saints shall judge the world?" (I Cor. 6:1-2.) "Not rendering evil for evil, or railing for railing: but contrariwise blessing." (I Pet. 3:9.) "Let your conversation be without covetousness." (Heb. 13:5.) "But let your yea be yea; and your nay, nay; lest ye fall into condemnation." (Jas. 5:12.)

The whole gospel of Christ is a call to peace and brotherhood—peace and self-control within; kindness, gentleness, courtesy, and consideration to all without. This lesson is too deeply written in the Christian conscience to need further treament. We call our Lord the "Prince of Peace."

The last clause in this rule, the haggling over prices or driving for a close bargain in buying or selling, is aimed at the selfishness of the sharp trader. Those who use many words in buying or selling are not so anxious to arrive at a just price as to overcome the other party by superior mental adroitness or pressure. What the Christian must seek is fairness in all such dealings—fairness for himself, fairness for the other party.

RULE SIX

[Against] the buying or selling goods that have not paid the duty

SCRIPTURAL BASIS: "Provide things honest in the sight of all men." (Rom. 12:17.) "Render therefore unto Caesar the things which are Caesar's." (Matt. 22:21.) "Render therefore to all their dues." (Rom. 13:7.)

At the time these rules were written, the levying of duty on imported goods was something comparatively new. English people, who traditionally were used to free trade, bitterly resented the idea that the government should tax any of their possessions which they brought into their country. But now it is universally conceded that the government has a right to levy tariffs on imports, and good citizens recognize this everywhere. Every smuggler robs his country and stands as a thief before Almighty God. So do those who defraud their nation by cheating it of its rightful taxes, making fraudulent returns to the income-tax office, and so on. One has no more right to rob the government—or a city or a corporation, for that matter—than to rob a private individual.

RULE SEVEN

[Against] the giving or taking of things on usury —that is, unlawful interest

SCRIPTURAL BASIS: "Lord, who shall abide in thy tabernacle?—who shall dwell in thy holy hill? . . . He that putteth not out his money to usury, nor taketh reward against the innocent." (Ps. 15:1, 5.) "That no man go beyond and defraud his brother." (I Thess. 4:6.)

The Hebrew and Christian view that prevailed for many centuries was that any interest charged for the use of money was "usury" and wrong. But in the clearer view that came with the awakening of the modern world and the necessary expansion of trade and credit, it was seen that the rent of money (interest), like the rent of land or of houses, could be charged properly and accepted, provided such interest was fair and there was no taking advantage of the oppressed.

Wesley, in writing this rule, explained usury as "unlawful interest." The practice forbidden is to receive more for a loan than such loan is worth, measured not only by the law of the land, but by the higher law of the Golden Rule.

RULE EIGHT

[Against] uncharitable or unprofitable conversation; particularly speaking evil of magistrates or ministers

The Bible truly says the "tongue is a fire." More harm is done by idle talking than this world dreams of. Even greater harm is done by speaking evil of persons when they are not present to defend themselves, or by innuendoes which besmudge character. A famous authority once observed that the talebearer and the listener to such tales should both be hanged—one by the tongue, the other by the ear.

RULE NINE

[Against] doing to others as we would not they should do unto us

This really is a negative statement of the Golden Rule and speaks for itself.

RULE TEN

[Against] doing what we know is not for the glory of God, as: the putting on of gold and costly apparel

SCRIPTURAL BASIS: "Whose adorning let it not be that outward adorning of plaiting the hair, and of wearing of gold, or of putting on of apparel." (I Pet. 3:3.) "I will . . . that women adorn themselves in modest apparel, . . . not with braided hair, or gold, or pearls, or costly array." (I Tim. 2:8, 9.)

Needless extravagance in dress and useless and showy ornamentation are forbidden by this rule. It was written in a day when English class distinctions were clear-cut and deep. Those who were then known as "gentlemen" or "ladies" had to dress in a certain fine way in keeping with their station. The common people—and into this class most Methodists belonged—were not expected to put on fine garments, for to do so was considered pretense and hypocrisy. John Wesley energetically forbade his people to "ape the gentleman," as he expressed it.

Christians today do not consider quiet adornment as wrong. Nevertheless, while we have departed somewhat from the strict plainness of early days, it still is true that Christian people have no right to spend on ornaments and unnecessary luxuries anything more than a modest fraction of their means. We could do with much more self-denial today. As long as there are poverty and hunger in the world, as long as there are those in desperate need, we have no right to spend too much upon ourselves. "You are not to adorn yourselves on the outside with braids of hair and ornaments of gold"—so Moffatt translates the verse from I Peter which was given above. To this Goodspeed adds, "Yours must be the inner beauty of character."

RULE ELEVEN

[Against] the taking of such diversions as cannot be used in the name of the Lord Jesus

SCRIPTURAL BASIS: "Be not conformed to this world." (Rom. 12:2.) "Know ye not that the friendship of the world is enmity with God?" (Jas. 4:4.) "Love not the world, neither the things that are in the world." (I John 2:15.)

It is to be noticed that this rule does not cite the diversions which are forbidden. Time after time in the life of the church various popular amusements have been blacklisted.

For a long time the dance, the theater, the circus, were named as worldly amusements unfit for Christian participation. But Christian liberty allows each individual to determine in the sight of God what is right for him. Wholesome recreation has a part in life, and there are many amusements which not only are innocent in themselves, but build up character and refit one for the daily task. But whatever one feels to be wrong for him to do, *to him that particular thing is wrong*.

RULE TWELVE

[Against] the singing those songs, or reading those books which do not tend to the knowledge or love of God

SCRIPTURAL BASIS: "Be not deceived: evil communications corrupt good manners." (I Cor. 15:33.) "Speaking to yourselves in psalms and hymns and spiritual songs, singing and making melody in your heart to the Lord." (Eph. 5:19.) "I count all things but loss for the excellency of the knowledge of Christ Jesus my Lord." (Phil. 3:8.) "And whatsoever ye do in word or deed, do all in the name of the Lord Jesus." (Col. 3:17.)

This rule sets one on the positive way to righteousness by blocking out everything which does not help along that way. It was written to make all time count for God and strictly interpreted would forbid all secular reading and music. Certainly the enjoyment of song and the reading of books which are not harmful in themselves have both recreational and character-building value. On the other hand there are books, plays, and pictures that are definitely harmful. Between these extremes there is the middle register of amusements that are neither very edifying nor positively harmful. Each Christian must decide for himself how much God-given time he shall draw upon for such diversions. All of life must be made to count for righteousness.

RULE THIRTEEN

[Against] softness and needless self-indulgence

SCRIPTURAL BASIS: "Then said Jesus unto his disciples, If any man will come after me, let him deny himself, and take up his cross, and follow me." (Matt. 16:24.)

Self-control, self-denial—these are familiar words in the Christian vocabulary. If athletes, such as prize fighters and distance runners, submit to rigorous training to obtain the fading laurels of earthly victory, surely the people of God can put away ease and self-indulgence and grow in moral stamina as well as grace. "God give us a hardened soldiery," an old Methodist bishop prayed once as he ordained his preachers. No ease-loving people, comfortable and well fixed, can impress the world. "Except I shall see in his hands the print of the nails," said Thomas, "I will not believe."

People would believe our witness more today if we denied ourselves more, gave more, and so appeared to be more in earnest. We cannot spend vast sums upon our homes, our travel, our comfort, our ease in life, without losing something in our own character, as well as a great opportunity to influence the characters of others.

RULE FOURTEEN

[Against] laying up treasure upon earth

SCRIPTURAL BASIS: "Lay not up for yourselves treasures upon earth, where moth and rust doth corrupt, and where thieves break through and steal: but lay up for yourselves treasures in heaven, where neither moth nor rust doth corrupt, and where thieves do not break through nor steal: for where your treasure is, there will your heart be also." (Matt. 6:19-21.)

The positive side of this injunction—to lay up treasures in heaven—could be emphasized even more than the negative.

There is no wrong in providing for oneself and one's own in all needful things. Every Christian is expected to pull his own weight in making a living and have something left over, if possible, to pull the weight of others. Paul declared that if a man did not provide for his own and especially for those of his own household, he is "worse than an infidel" (I Tim. 5:8).

Christianity always has taught diligence, thrift, frugality, and that the laborer is worthy of his hire. But earthly values are never to supplant the coinage of heaven. Wesley's rule for managing money is to be remembered: "Make all you can; save all you can; give all you can." Every Christian has been entrusted with earthly goods in order that he may use them for heavenly purposes. It is possible to deal so in earthly treasures as to receive heavenly dividends.

RULE FIFTEEN

[Against] **borrowing without a probability of paying; or taking up goods without a probability of paying for them**

SCRIPTURAL BASIS: "The wicked borroweth, and payeth not again." (Ps. 37:21.) "Render unto all their dues." (Rom. 18:7.) "Recompense to no man evil for evil. Provide things honest in the sight of all men." (Rom. 12:17.) "Owe no man any thing, but to love one another." (Rom. 13:8.)

Taking chances in matters of financial outlay is forbidden by a common-sense Christianity. To be sure, misfortune in business sometimes overtakes a good man as well as a bad one, and there is risk in all enterprise; but the hasty assumption of heavy obligations, or reckless borrowing, is wrong in the sight of both man and God.

Up to this point we have been following the negative injunctions of the General Rules—what we must *not* do. We now come to the positive rules.

The Positive Rules

"It is expected of all who continue in these societies that they shall continue to evidence their desire of salvation":

RULE SIXTEEN

By doing good; by being in every kind merciful after their power; as they have opportunity, doing good of every possible sort, and, as far as possible, to all men

SCRIPTURAL BASIS: "Trust in the Lord, and do good." (Ps. 37:3.) "To do good and to communicate forget not." (Heb. 13:16.) "Blessed are the merciful: for they shall obtain mercy." (Matt. 5:7.) "To him that knoweth to do good, and doeth it not, to him it is sin." (Jas. 4:17.) "As we have therefore opportunity, let us do good unto all men." (Gal. 6:10.)

This is the broad injunction which everyone with the desire to lead a Christian life should have continually before him. Opportunities are open to us on all sides for the doing of good—to ourselves, to our families, to our fellow men, to the world in which we live. There is no way to outline the myriad series of opportunities which come before us each day, but the alert Christian will be able to discern and take advantage of each one.

When the Lord gave his picture of the final judgment, he made his commendation, as well as his condemnation, to depend upon the feeding of the hungry, the visiting of the sick and those in prison, and the doing of good to needy people. "Inasmuch as ye have done it unto one of the least of these my brethren, ye have done it unto me."

The whole matter of kindliness and of Christian charity was thus forever laid upon the hearts of God's people. What is to be remembered is not so much that we must have a sincere intent to do good deeds, but that we shall actually (1) see opportunities and (2) follow them out in acts of service that benefit our fellow men.

RULE SEVENTEEN

[Doing good] to their bodies, of the ability of which God giveth, by giving food to the hungry, by clothing the naked, by visiting or helping them that are sick or in prison

SCRIPTURAL BASIS: "Then shall the King say unto them on his right hand, Come, ye blessed of my Father, inherit the kingdom prepared for you from the foundation of the world: for I was ahungered, and ye gave me meat: I was thirsty, and ye gave me drink: I was a stranger, and ye took me in: naked, and ye clothed me: I was sick, and ye visited me: I was in prison, and ye came unto me. . . . Inasmuch as ye have done it unto one of the least of these my brethren, ye have done it unto me." (Matt. 25:34-36, 40.)

RULE EIGHTEEN

[Doing good] to their souls, by instructing, reproving or exhorting all we have any intercourse with; trampling under foot that enthusiastic doctrine, that "we are not to do good unless our hearts be free to it."

SCRIPTURAL BASIS: "Reprove, rebuke, exhort with all longsuffering and doctrine." (II Tim. 4:2.) "Exhort one another daily." (Heb. 3:13.) "Them that sin rebuke before all, that others also may fear." (I Tim. 5:20.) "Ye are the salt of the earth . . . ye are the light of the world." (Matt. 5:13, 14.)

The two rules above are so obvious that they need only to be put down to be approved. To do good to the bodies and souls of men—this has been the law of Christianity ever since Jesus, the great physician, sent his disciples out to teach and to heal. In a world where the have-nots outnumber the haves, where there is a desperate need on every side, the ancient command to "do good unto all men" is never to be forgotten.

"No man hungers but that I hunger; no man thirsts but that I thirst." This is the true Christian attitude.

The Methodist passion for social justice, so strong today, stems directly from the principle laid down in these rules. Methodism is not, and never has been, the private cultivation of a mere inner spirituality. Rather it is the dynamic outgrowing of the Christian spirit into every area of life where good can be done to the souls and bodies of men. Its aggressive attack upon evil, public and private, caused one writer to describe Methodism as an "invasive encampment upon the field of the world."

A word of explanation is due here regarding the last expression of Rule Eighteen: "trampling under foot that enthusiastic doctrine . . . not to do good unless our hearts be free to it." Certain sincere, but unrealistic, Christians at the time of John Wesley taught that if one did not feel like doing a good deed, it was wrong for him to make any move to do it. They refused to partake of the sacrament unless they felt that they were perfectly prepared, and even believed it wrong to pray unless moved to it.

Wesley and the early Methodists repudiated these strange ideas with all the force they had. Wesley said that when one did not feel like going to church or taking Communion or praying, that was the very time when he should do these things. Christianity always moves forward by "trampling under foot" any feelings which interfere with duty. We are to be guided not by our immediate impulses, but by what we know to be right.

RULE NINETEEN

By doing good, especially to them that are of the household of faith or groaning so to be; employing them preferably to others; buying one of another; helping

each other in business; and so much the more because the world will love its own and them *only*

SCRIPTURAL BASIS: "As we have therefore opportunity, let us do good unto all men, especially unto them who are of the household of faith." (Gal. 6:10.) "Be kindly affectioned one to another with brotherly love; in honour preferring one another; . . . distributing to the necessity of saints; given to hospitality." (Rom. 12:10, 13.)

Christian fellowship and mutual helpfulness are taught all through the Bible. Every Christian group is expected to be a brotherhood, and the Church itself has sometimes been called the "communion of the saints."

In the New Testament the Church is regarded as a family— the "household of God." Such a household must have affection to bind the family circle together, obedience holding all to the rules of the home, and a loving attitude tying brother to brother and sister to sister.

In a practical way this rule stresses the duty of Christians to stand by one another in the economic and social undertakings of life. Where a brother churchman has a store or conducts a business, we should buy from him and patronize those who belong to our fellowship. To be sure, the Christian brotherhood is not a partnership for economic and social profit, although there are persons who join the church in order to gain temporally. Jesus himself had some who followed him for the "loaves and the fishes." But as the rule here reminds us, the "world will love its own" (worldly people stick together), and so should Christians. "We are a colony of heaven." Paul beautifully expressed it (Phil. 3:20 Moffatt).

RULE TWENTY

[Shall so live] by all possible diligence and frugality that the gospel be not blamed

SCRIPTURAL BASIS: "Not slothful in business; fervent in spirit; serving the Lord." (Rom. 12:11.) "If any provide not for his own, and specially for those of his own house, he hath denied the faith, and is worse than an infidel." (I Tim. 5:8.)

This rule is simple—likewise direct. Diligence means care and attention to details, and an earnest busyness about the affairs of life; frugality means saving ("making it do"), and this not wholly for ourselves but to have more for all.

Every Christian is therefore expected (as was said of Rule Fourteen), to pull his own weight in the world and then to help others pull theirs. The Bible has no patience with economic parasites, or those who try to get without giving. In a day when the idea has grown that people are to be taken care of by the government or by a collectivist society, the robust ideal of this rule (which was also that of our early American forebears) is to be remembered. "If any provide not for his own, . . . he hath denied the faith."

RULE TWENTY-ONE

[Shall live] by running with patience the race that is set before them, denying themselves, and taking up their cross daily, submitting to bear the reproach of Christ, to be as the filth and offscouring of the world; and looking that men should say all manner of evil of them falsely, for the Lord's sake

SCRIPTURAL BASIS: "Seeing we also are compassed about with so great a cloud of witnesses, let us lay aside every weight, and the sin which doth so easily beset us, and let us run with patience the race that is set before us." (Heb. 12:1.) "If any man will come after me, let him deny himself, and take up his cross, and follow me." (Matt. 16:24.) "We are made as the filth of the world, and are the offscouring of all things unto this day." (I Cor. 4:13.) "Blessed are ye, when men shall revile you, and persecute you, and shall say all manner of evil against you falsely, for my sake." (Matt. 5:11.)

This rule requires the cultivation of patience, a virtue which is not easy to come by. It sets the pace not for a quick race but for enduring whatever life has to bring. Our business in life is to grow in grace as followers of the Lord. To do so we must not only have patience but be ready to endure sorrow, expect opposition, and, if need be, accept poverty and the reverses of fortune. In every life there is a cross which must be taken up daily. God has not promised us happiness, but he has promised us the peace which passeth all understanding—the deep assurance that whatever happens, his goodness and mercy are over all his children.

The third division of the General Rules outlines positive religious duties.

Positive Religious Duties

At this point comes in the churchliness of Methodism. Up to now the rules laid down might be taken by any pious person or sectarian group as proper guidance on what to do and what not to do. But the General Rules were not given simply to guide a "society" but members of the Church of God—the Church with its preaching, its sacraments, its ordered ministries. The rules that here follow are a direct contradiction to the idea that Methodism is simply a set of pious, personal regulations. Over all its doctrine, organization, and discipline is The Church—holy, catholic, eternal—in which every Methodist must have his being if he is to be a Methodist at all.

"It is expected of all who desire to continue in these societies that they shall continue to evidence their desire of salvation":

96

RULE TWENTY-TWO

By attending upon all the ordinances of God; such [as] the public worship of God

SCRIPTURAL BASIS: "One thing have I desired of the Lord, that will I seek after; that I may dwell in the house of the Lord all the days of my life, to behold the beauty of the Lord, and to enquire in his temple." (Ps. 27:4.) "Not forsaking the assembling of ourselves together, as the manner of some is." (Heb. 10:25.)

RULE TWENTY-THREE

[Should attend] the ministry of the Word, either read or expounded

SCRIPTURAL BASIS: Christ instituted his ministry and said, "Go ye therefore, and teach all nations, . . . teaching them to observe all things whatsoever I have commanded you: and, lo, I am with you alway even unto the end of the world." (Matt. 28:19, 20.) "So then faith cometh by hearing, and hearing by the word of God." (Rom. 10:17.) "But whoso looketh into the perfect law of liberty, and continueth therein, he being not a forgetful hearer, but a doer of the work, this man shall be blessed in his deed." (Jas. 1:25.)

These two rules naturally belong together, for one is the extension of the other. Christians must attend public worship for their souls' health. It refits them for life, feeds them spiritually, and is the God-given method whereby the Church holds and nurtures its own. Absence from public worship represents a spiritual loss, and willful and continued absence always ends with a *forgotten Church and a forgotten God*. Every Methodist should attend church when services are held in his church on Sunday, and every pastor who fails to remind his people of this, their duty, is remiss in his.

Church attendance is not intended to be a spectator sport in which passive worshipers hear the delivery of a sermon and watch a paid choir conduct music. Participation on the part of each is more than duty; it becomes a genuine gladness when entered into sincerely. The responsive readings, the unison prayers, and especially the hymns of the church—in these our people are expected to participate and are glad to do so.

RULE TWENTY-FOUR

[Must not neglect] the Supper of the Lord

SCRIPTURAL BASIS: (For this and our Church's teachings regarding the Lord's Supper and its observance, see pages 140-47.)

The sacrament of the Lord's Supper has always been to every Christian a true means of grace. God's table is set and ready. His people must "draw near with faith"; and when they do, they literally take the sacrament, as our ritual has it, "to [their] comfort."

RULE TWENTY-FIVE

[Must not neglect] family and private prayer

SCRIPTURAL BASIS: "As for me and my house, we will serve the Lord." (Josh. 24:15.) "When thou prayest, enter into thy closet, and when thou hast shut thy door, pray to thy Father which is in secret; and thy Father which seest in secret shall reward thee openly." (Matt. 6:6.) "Pray without ceasing. In every thing give thanks." (I Thess. 5:17-18.)

The old custom of holding family prayers has been discarded in most modern Methodist homes, and the loss is very great. Many a man or woman living today in the fullness of Christian maturity looks back with gratitude to family prayers in his own home. Just as every child has the right to be wellborn, so every child should have the right to be surrounded continually by Christian influences—by grace at the table and a brief period of home devotion. Admittedly it is difficult to find the time for this stated prayer in a home today, but it can be done and means much in Christian life. Short scripture reading and prayer at the breakfast hour is the way many Methodist families manage this.

The Bible has much to say about praying in solitude, and our Lord himself set an example here. If Jesus found it necessary to pray, his disciples surely need it far more. Much is heard today about peace of mind and peace of soul, but the peace that the gospel knows is that inner spiritual assurance that always comes to those who make their way regularly into the secret of God's presence by meditation and prayer. No matter how busy the schedule or how rushed the life, time must be taken for this.

RULE TWENTY-SIX

[Must not neglect] searching the Scriptures

SCRIPTURAL BASIS: "I will meditate in thy precepts, and have respect unto thy ways. I will delight myself in thy statutes: I will not forget thy word." (Ps. 119:15-16.) "Search the scriptures; for in them ye think ye have eternal life: and they are they which testify of me." (John 5:39.)

There is a personal message in the Book of God which speaks directly to the heart of every man. Against all doubters the Bible is its own best witness. Truth has a self-evidencing power nowhere stronger felt than when the pages of sacred writ are studied and read. There are today excellent commentaries and a wealth of reverent interpretations which help us to understand the truth of God's Word. These echo the words of the Psalmist: "Send out thy light and thy truth: let them lead me; let them bring me unto thy holy hill" (Ps. 43:3).

"The Bible is a rock of diamonds, a chain of pearls, the sword of the Spirit," said Dr. Watson; "a chart by which the Christian sails to eternity; the map by which he daily walks;

the sun-dial by which he sets his life; the balances in which he weighs his action."

It has been said that no one can live in sin and read the Bible ten minutes every day. One action blocks out the other. Let God's people read continually the sacred Book, and it truly will be a "lamp unto [their] feet," opening more and more into the light of the perfect day.

RULE TWENTY-SEVEN

[Must not neglect] fasting or abstinence

SCRIPTURAL BASIS: Fasting has been a method of religious observance throughout the ages. It was prescribed in the Old Testament; it was observed in the New. "As they ministered to the Lord, and fasted, the Holy Ghost said, Separate me Barnabas and Saul for the work whereunto I have called them. And when they had fasted and prayed, and laid their hands on them, they sent them away." (Acts 13:2-3.) "And when they had ordained them elders in every church, and had prayed with fasting, they commended them to the Lord, on whom they believed." (Acts 14:23.)

We do not put as much emphasis upon the need of fasting as did our fathers. The old theory was that it was spiritually healthy to mortify, that is, to kill, the impulses of the body. Modern Christians are inclined to believe that the needs of the body should neither obtrude themselves unduly nor be crushed unduly. For many people there is a spiritual value in abstaining from food at certain times; for others there is the feeling that since abstention from food is a break in the ordered regimen of the day, thus slackening efficiency by that much, it need not be insisted upon so strongly.

Nevertheless, just as when we are under some high emotional strain, as in danger or in great sorrow, and we do not feel like touching food, so when we desire earnestly to find our way into some great spiritual experience, we can wisely push from us the satisfaction of material wants. Concerning fasting, let each one be fully persuaded in his own mind. We appreciate the fact that occasionally in our nation's history national as well as church leaders have called for days of fasting and prayer, that all may take occasion to think more deeply upon eternal verities.

John Wesley ended the General Rules with an impressive statement given here in its entirety:

These are the General Rules of our societies; all of which we are taught of God to observe, even in his written Word, which is the only rule, and the sufficient rule, both of our faith and practice. And all these we know his Spirit writes on truly awakened hearts. If there be any among us who observes them not, who habitually breaks any of them, let it be known unto them who watch over that soul as they who must give an account. We will admonish him of the error of his ways. We will bear with him for a season. But, if then he repent not, he hath no more place among us. We have delivered our own souls.

So John Wesley closed the rules of the Methodist canon.

CHAPTER FIVE

Organization

To EACH METHODIST LAYMAN the organization of his own local church seems more important than the big overall structure of Methodism as a whole. This is understandable. He lives his life in the local church, attends its services, contributes to its finances, and if he is a steward, trustee, or other church officer, has a direct part to play in its work. He knows in a general way that The Methodist Church is a big institution with bishops and boards, conferences and huge budgets. But too often the average layman feels that the Methodist organization is too complicated for him to understand; and as he does not necessarily have to understand it, he is inclined to dismiss it from further thought. But this is neither sensible nor correct. It is not too difficult to understand the Methodist organization, and every Methodist should know in a general way how it functions.

The Methodist Church, though large, is a closely knit organization. The unit of the organization is the local church, or "charge," as it has always been called in Methodism. A charge may be one or more local churches. If it is one church, it is a "station charge," or "station"; if more than one church, the group is a "circuit" and is called a "circuit charge."

Charges are grouped geographically into "districts," each supervised by a minister known as the district superintendent.

Districts in turn compose a larger grouping, the Annual Conference. This is presided over by a bishop.

Annual Conferences make up larger regional divisions known as jurisdictions, of which there are six in the United States.

The General Conference

This is the supreme governing and lawmaking body of Methodism and one of the most influential church bodies in the world. It meets every four years and manages and directs the affairs of the church. It is composed of ministers and laymen in equal numbers, all of whom are elected as delegates by the Annual Conferences.

Every Annual Conference is allowed to elect one ministerial member for every 70 ministers of the electing conference; the laymen elect an equal number of laymen. For instance, if the Newark Annual Conference is permitted to elect three ministerial members (because it has something over 210 preacher members), then the laymen of the Newark Conference will elect three laymen, making a total delegation of six.

No one can belong to the General Conference unless he has been elected to it by one of the Annual Conferences of Methodism. There are no appointive nor ex-officio members. The bishops preside over the General Conference but are not members of it.

The business of the General Conference is to revise the book of *Discipline,* to make laws, and determine all sorts of important matters having to do with the ongoing of the Church.

The General Conference at its opening session first hears a comprehensive report from all the bishops—the "Episcopal Address." This address may be likened to the President's message to each new Congress on the state of the union. The General Conference then proceeds to do its work by repealing or amending old laws, by passing new ones, and by determining the course of the Church for the next four years.

It has full powers to:

1. Define and fix the powers of Annual Conferences, Mission Conferences, District and Quarterly Conferences, and smaller church bodies.

2. Define and fix the powers of the bishops, ministers, and church members where these have not already been determined by the Constitution of the Church.

3. Revise the hymnbook and ritual of the church when necessary and provide forms for worship in accordance with Methodist usage and custom.

4. Plan and in large measure direct all the connectional enterprises, such as missions, education, publishing interests, hospitals, ministerial training, and the like.

5. Set up a budget for the whole church for the coming four years and determine how this is to be raised and administered.

The General Conference has sweeping powers to "enact such other legislation as may be necessary, subject to the limitations and restrictions of the Constitution of the church."

There are some things the General Conference cannot do:

1. Change the Articles of Religion or the standards of Methodist doctrine.

2. Destroy the episcopacy (administration by bishops).

3. Change the General Rules of the church.

4. Do away with the privileges of a church trial as prescribed in the *Discipline*.

5. Appropriate the produce of the Publishing House for any other cause than the support of the retired preachers and the widows and orphans of preachers.

6. Elect bishops, as bishops are now elected by the Jurisdictional Conferences.

7. Change the constitution of The Methodist Church, though it can *recommend* a change by a two-thirds vote. (Such a change, to be effected, will then require the consent of two thirds[1] of the members of all the Annual Conferences who shall later vote, conference by conference.)

The Jurisdictional Conference

The Jurisdictional Conference is a new feature in Methodism. At the time of church union in 1939 The Methodist Church inside the United States was divided for administrative purposes into regions known as jurisdictions. Five of these are geographic, and one is racial.

The five geographic jurisdictions of The Methodist Church are as follows: the North Central, the Northeastern, the South Central, the Southeastern, and the Western. Each of these blocks off a certain large section of the United States and unites the Annual Conferences of that section into a jurisdiction. Negro Annual Conferences are grouped together to form a jurisdiction of their own, irrespective of geographic location. This is known as the Central Jurisdiction.

The Jurisdictional Conference meets once every four years within a month or two after the session of the General Conference. Each Jurisdictional Conference is composed of the elected representatives of the Annual Conferences who have been members of the General Conference immediately preceding, plus a proportionate number of additional ministers and laymen, so there shall be all together in the Jurisdictional Conference one ministerial delegate for every thirty ministers of the electing conference—and, of course, an equal number of laymen.

[1] It would require three fourths of all the members of the **Annual Conferences** present and voting to change an Article of Religion.

The great duty of the Jurisdictional Conference is to elect the bishops and the members of most of the boards and general agencies of the church. It must also plan the general program of church work to be carried out within the jurisdiction during the coming four years.

The number of bishops to be elected by the respective Jurisdictional Conferences depends upon the number of church members enrolled in the jurisdiction. Every jurisdiction having 500,000 church members is allowed to have a minimum of four bishops, and for each additional 500,000 church members or two thirds thereof any jurisdiction shall be entitled to elect one additional bishop.[2]

The election of bishops and board members was vested in the Jurisdictional Conference in order that the different sections of the country and the Central Jurisdiction might have proportionate representation upon all the boards and in the episcopacy.

Central Conferences

Central Conferences are in effect Jurisdictional Conferences outside the United States and its territories. The Annual Conferences in a certain land or region, as, for instance, northern Europe or Latin America, meet each four years in a Central Conference, as it is called. Such conferences have important powers of election and direction with regard to their own affairs. Central Conferences elect bishops when the General Conference empowers them to do so in each instance. Central Conference bishops are elected in most instances for

[2] An exception is made in the case of those jurisdictions where there may be more than 70,000 square miles in each episcopal area as an average. Such jurisdictions are allowed to have four bishops for the first 400,000 members and one additional bishop for each additional 400,000.

a term of office rather than for life, as is the case with the bishops of the American jurisdictions. Central Conference bishops, however, have all the powers of Methodist bishops in every essential.

The Annual Conference

The Annual Conference is the basic body of Methodism. It consists of all the traveling preachers who live within a certain territory; and of lay members, one of whom is elected from every charge in the conference area.

Ministers when once admitted to an Annual Conference become members of it for life. They are known as "traveling preachers." Every ministerial member of the conference must be appointed to some charge by the bishop. Ministers can be transferred, that is, moved from one Annual Conference to another; but no minister can be refused an appointment as long as he is a member of an Annual Conference.

An Annual Conference can "locate" a ministerial member by formal vote when he does not impress the conference as being suitable or qualified for the traveling ministry. This makes him a local preacher again. A minister may locate voluntarily by requesting that he be allowed to drop out of the itinerant, or traveling, ministry and resume the status of a local preacher.

The lay members of the Annual Conference are elected by their local churches. Each charge is allowed to elect one delegate only. Lay delegates serve for a term of one year or of four years, depending on the way their Annual Conference decides this should be.

The Annual Conference has the following important powers:

1. To determine what ministers shall be admitted to its membership and who may be ordained.

2. To vote on all constitutional amendments as these may be proposed by the General Conference.

3. To elect delegates to the General and Jurisdictional Conferences once every four years.

4. To have all other rights which have not been delegated to the General Conference under the constitution.

This last is an extremely important provision. It keeps all reserved powers in the hands of the Annual Conferences rather than in the hands of the General Conference, as was the case before church union in 1939.

There are 148 Annual Conferences in The Methodist Church, many of them outside the United States.

A bishop presides over each session of the Annual Conference; and when acting in this capacity, he is termed the "conference president." He must see that the business of the conference is properly managed and that the age-old Methodist Annual Conference questions—some of them out of the old *General Minutes* of Wesley's first conferences—are asked and answered.

The Annual Conference, although it has a lay member from each charge, is historically a preachers' conference. Its chief duties have to do with the ministry and its work—with ministers' reports, ministers' characters, ministers' superannuation, ministers' admission on trial, ministers' ordination, and most important of all, the stationing of the ministers (reading the appointments).

To be sure, there are other matters of high import which each Annual Conference must act upon, and the lay members have an important part to play. There are many committees to report, many plans made for work through the year, many causes and interests to be looked after.

Membership in an Annual Conference is considered a high privilege, and rightly so. Conferences take pride in their accomplishments and personnel, and vie with one another in the work of Methodism. Every Annual Conference is governed by the same rules and conducts its business in the same way as every other Annual Conference, but there are characteristic differences which give to each a certain individuality.

The actions and influence of a Methodist Annual Conference have great weight in its own region. Other Christian denominations are influenced by "what the Methodists do," and the social and political life of a whole state feels the impact of the Methodist conference.

The District Conference

A District Conference is held once a year in every district superintendent's area if the Annual Conference containing that district so orders. If an Annual Conference decides not to have District Conferences, none are held; if it decides to have District Conferences, these are held year after year in all the districts of that particular Annual Conference.

This difference came about at unification in 1939. The former Methodist Episcopal Church, South, had District Conferences over all its connection and found them very helpful. The Methodist Episcopal Church used them rarely. Leaving it to each Annual Conference to decide whether or not to have District Conferences, any tension regarding this difference was done away. The southern conferences have continued the District Conferences without a break, and many of the Annual Conferences of the former Methodist Episcopal Church have created District Conferences and find them helpful.

The District Conference consists of all the preachers who are serving charges in the district, together with all local preachers, and a certain number of lay delegates elected from each charge as well as certain district officers. It is presided over by the district superintendent, who is expected to take the occasion to check up on the progress of the work in his district and to see that the program of the church is properly presented and supported. The various causes of the general church are represented at the District Conference, often by visiting general church officials, who are enabled thus to give the District Conference a view of the progress and purposes of the church's work.

An important duty of the District Conference is to take final action on the licensing of properly qualified persons to preach.

The Quarterly Conference

We now come to that part of the Methodist organization which is of special importance to members of the local church —their Quarterly Conference.

The Quarterly Conference is the governing body of the local church or charge. Belonging to the Quarterly Conference are all the officials of the local church—the pastor, assistant pastors if any, stewards, trustees, local preachers if any, superintendent of the church school, the president of the Woman's Society of Christian Service, and a number of other specified officers.

The Quarterly Conference meets every three months— hence the term "quarterly." In some instances the second and third Quarterly Conferences of any Annual Conference year can be omitted. The *first* Quarterly Conference and the *last* one must always be held.

Presiding over the Quarterly Conference is the district superintendent.[3] At its sessions he asks for regular reports from the pastor and from the other officials and committees of the charge. The *Discipline* directs the district superintendent as to what questions he must ask and what reports he must

---

[3] The office of district superintendent is discussed on page 124.

call for at each session. This is a uniform procedure over all of Methodism, so that not only is the business of each local church reviewed and brought up to date at Quarterly Conference time, but it is done the same way in every Methodist church. The questions asked in Tennessee at the first Quarterly Conference of every year are the same questions asked in the first Methodist Quarterly Conference in Montana or in southern Texas or anywhere else.

The Quarterly Conference has important *executive* powers. It decides what the pastor's salary shall be, what amount of money it shall accept as its share of general church work, and how the business affairs of the local church are to be managed. It can buy or build, sell or mortgage, a church building or parsonage and in general take care of all property matters according to the *Discipline* of the Church and the laws of the respective states.

Formerly the Quarterly Conference of the charge—which might be composed of several circuit churches—dealt with the property of each one of its local churches. This caused difficulties, and in 1952 it was provided that each local church on a circuit, no matter how small, must have its own Church Quarterly Conference to take care of its special property rights.

The Quarterly Conference has important *electoral* powers. It elects the delegate who is to represent the charge at the Annual Conference, the delegates to the District Conference, the stewards of the church, the trustees who are to hold in trust the church property.

It recommends to the proper licensing committee those who wish to become preachers; and unless a person has a recommendation from his own Quarterly Conference, he cannot be licensed to preach.

Certain important commissions and committees are set up by the Quarterly Conference to assist in carrying on its work. Chief among these are four: the Commission on Membership and Evangelism, the Commission on Education, the Commission on Missions, the Commission on Finance.

Because of the importance of these commissions in each local church, space must be taken to describe them.

The COMMISSION ON MEMBERSHIP AND EVANGELISM has as its great task the promotion of the program of evangelism within the church and the community. It must also seek out the inactive and negligent members and vitally concern itself with the entire program of spiritual well-being in the local church. It ties in closely with the General and Annual Conference boards of evangelism and has a primary responsibility for reaching the unsaved and unchurched in the community.

Every member of the commission must be a member of The Methodist Church. The pastor, the secretary of spiritual life of the Woman's Society of Christian Service, the church-school superintendent, and certain others named by the *Discipline* must always be on this commission.

The COMMISSION ON EDUCATION determines policies for the church school and gives general direction to all the educational work of the local church. It has responsibilities toward enlisting and training the necessary officers and teachers for the church school and of electing them to their respective positions. A number of other duties are specified for this commission by the *Discipline*, all of them having to do with the cause of Christian education in the local church. The membership of the commission is carefully outlined in the *Discipline*. It of course is expected to co-operate with the Annual Conference Board of Education and with the Division of the Local Church of the General Board of Education.

A COMMISSION ON MISSIONS must also be organized in each local church. This must be composed of not less than three persons and as many more as the Quarterly Conference may determine. It is the duty of this commission to provide for the diffusion of missionary information and literature, and for planning in co-operation with the Woman's Society of Christian Service other moves for furthering the cause of missions at home and abroad. This commission ties in with the General and Annual Conference Boards of Missions, co-operating with these agencies in their general plans and programs.

The COMMISSION ON FINANCE is the last, but by no means the least, of the four commissions that every Quarterly Conference must create. Traditionally the chief responsibility of the officials in each local church has been to make proper provision for financial needs, including ministerial support. The Official Board of an earlier day acted chiefly as a committee on finance and so functioned most of the time. Under the present system the Commission on Finance, though elected by the Quarterly Conference, must work under the authority and direction of the Official Board.

By virtue of their respective offices the following must always belong to the Commission on Finance: pastor, church lay leader, financial secretary, church treasurer or treasurers, and chairman of the Commission on Missions. Such other members as the Quarterly Conference may determine may be added to it. In actual practice a large part of the Official Board—sometimes the whole board—is made the Commission on Finance.

The *Discipline* gives careful directions regarding the work of this commission. This includes setting up a budget for the local church in consultation with the pastor, and an active every-member canvass to secure pledges of support for the church.

As the church treasurer is a member of the Commission on Finance, much of its work must be cleared through him. This commission of course works directly under the authority of the Official Board.

While the above-described commissions are all created by the Quarterly Conference, they report to the Official Board. Their duties are specified rather minutely in the *Discipline;* and stewards, trustees, and local-church officials are expected to familiarize themselves with these duties.

It is an old Methodist principle that the Quarterly Conference has no quorum. It can transact its business no matter how small a number of members is present. However, it is necessary for the district superintendent to announce well in advance the time and place of a Quarterly Conference meeting, so that all members may have an opportunity to attend. Instances have been known where only the district superintendent and pastor were present, but nevertheless a legal Quarterly Conference was held.

No church property, however, can be mortgaged, sold, or conveyed by action of the Quarterly Conference unless at least ten days prior notice of such proposed action shall be given from the pulpit, together with the announcement of the time of holding the conference which will act on the matter.

If a Quarterly Conference does not wish to elect stewards and trustees by its own vote, it may direct that an Annual Church Conference shall be held in connection with the fourth Quarterly Conference to take care of these elections. Such a church conference, composed of all members of the church who are over eighteen years of age, shall thereupon meet and elect these church officials for the ensuing year. Many local churches prefer to elect their stewards and trustees in this manner.

The Official Board

An Official Board must be organized in every church in Methodism. It is composed of the pastor, the trustees, the stewards, and certain other church officials who are termed "ex-officio stewards." The last named, for example, the church-school superintendent, the president of the Woman's Society of Christian Service, and other specified persons, though not stewards by election, properly serve with the stewards as members of the Official Board.

The Official Board is the administrative agency of the Quarterly Conference and technically derives its power from that body. Practically, however, the Official Board is the real power in every Methodist church. This is because it meets monthly rather than quarterly (as does the Quarterly Conference); it is tightly integrated; it effectively controls all finances; and it is the cabinet of the pastor, working hand in glove with him at all times.

There is no chance for a conflict between the Official Board and the Quarterly Conference since the same people compose both. The Quarterly Conference is really the Official Board meeting the district superintendent once a quarter to report on its larger connectional responsibilities, and the Official Board is in effect the Quarterly Conference meeting as its own administrative agency.

The great duty of the Official Board is to manage the finances of the local church. The relation of the Board to the Commission on Finance elected by the Quarterly Conference has been mentioned. Some churches through the Quarterly Conference simply turn over the whole work of finance to the Official Board or direct the board itself to be the Commission on Finance. The *Discipline* prescribes in great detail how the finances of each local church are to be managed.

Beside its financial responsibilities the board has many minor administrative duties and creates special committees for such purposes as the need arises. It elects its own chairman (who may be the pastor), its vice-chairman, recording secretary, treasurer or treasurers, and the church lay leader. Its regular monthly meetings give it a chance to keep up all its obligations and to make plans for the future good of the church.

General Boards and Agencies

The Church creates a number of boards and smaller commissions and committees, each designed to carry on some special function of its work. The following features mark these: (1) Each is created by the General Conference, which prescribes its membership and duties, and provides for its support. (2) Most boards are incorporated, hold property, and manage their own affairs under the *Discipline's* direction. (3) Each board and commission has a paid staff with executives, secretaries, headquarters, and so on. Thus they function continuously carrying out the Church's manifold work.

Most boards are supported by the World Service Fund (page 165), and these are known as "world service agencies." The BOARD OF PUBLICATION, however, manages the METHODIST PUBLISHING HOUSE and is self-supporting (devoting its proceeds to retired ministers); while the METHODIST COMMITTEE FOR OVERSEAS RELIEF and the COMMISSION ON CHAPLAINS are supported by special offerings, the COMMISSION ON PUBLIC RELATIONS AND METHODIST INFORMATION by the General Administration Fund (page 165), and the WOMAN'S DIVISION of the Board of Missions raises its own funds (page 160).

The world service agencies are listed on page 168. For a complete study of the several boards and agencies (which this book does not undertake to make), see the *Discipline*.

The Judicial Council

In closing this chapter, it seems fitting to say something about a unique feature of Methodist organization—the Judicial Council and Methodist trial law. The Methodist Church has a complete judicial system outlined in the book of *Discipline*. This provides for the proper trial of church members and of ministers where charges affecting their character or official actions are brought against them in a formal way. It provides also for an appeal when the decisions of trial committees are against them. A Committee on Appeals is created in each jurisdiction in order to pass upon all cases properly referred to it. Its decisions are final.

The church also has as its supreme court a Judicial Council. This body is established by the constitution of the church and has the power to rule upon the constitutionality of any act of the General Conference. It is also the duty of the Council to hear all appeals from a bishop's decision when this is formally made in an Annual Conference and deals with a question of Methodist law. There is no appeal from the Judicial Council's decision. Its ruling at once establishes firm Methodist law.

The Judicial Council sits during the sessions of the General Conference, as well as at other stated times. When the General Conference passes a law which the Judicial Council considers a violation of the constitution of the church, the report of the Judicial Council declaring the measure unconstitutional at once nullifies the law in question. However, the General Conference can pass the measure again by a two-thirds vote and refer it to the Annual Conferences as a proposal to amend the constitution. As was previously stated in the paragraph dealing with constitutional amendments, if two thirds of the members of the Annual Conferences, present and voting, shall then approve the proposal, it will be declared adopted as constitutional law.

CHAPTER SIX

Ministry and Church Officials

THE METHODIST CHURCH believes in a "called ministry." That is, it believes that true ministers of Jesus Christ will have a "sense of oughtness" toward the preaching of the gospel, a sense of calling or mission. Therefore the church's process, when it licenses men to preach, then ordains them and gives them pulpits and pastorates, is motivated by the desire to find out first of all whether or not a man has been truly called of God. "How shall we try those who profess to be moved by the Holy Ghost to preach?" was John Wesley's carefully worded question, rephrased as a directive today in our *Discipline*. Wesley, and the church after him, outlined and put into effect various ways of trying and testing men.

Becoming a Minister

Let us follow the career of a typical Methodist preacher. A young man feels called to preach. After talking with his pastor and district superintendent, if he continues to hold this conviction, he then goes before his Quarterly Conference for its recommendation for license to preach. His case is stated to that conference, and usually his pastor or some friend in the conference seconds his request.

The Quarterly Conference (and all the committees and conferences which subsequently pass on his case) are expected to be on the lookout for two things: Has he *gifts*? Has he

118

grace? For there are pious Christian men who have no gifts for the preaching or pastoral ministry, and on the other hand there occasionally appear very gifted men who have no deep sense of mission and whose very profession is sometimes suspect.

Assuming, however, that a Quarterly Conference recommends a young man for a license to preach, he then goes before the District Committee on Ministerial Qualifications. This is composed of the district superintendent and five other ministers. If they are impressed by the applicant, they vote to license him to preach. They give him a parchment stating that he has authority to preach the gospel. This allows him to preach, and he is expected to preach whenever he is called upon to do so by his pastor or district superintendent. He has become a *local preacher.*

Local preachers are true ministers of the gospel, and Methodism owes much of its success to them. However, the church is under no obligation to furnish a local preacher with a pulpit or provide for his support. These men are expected to gain their livelihood in some other work or profession and to preach from time to time as opportunity presents itself.

Becoming a local preacher is for a young man usually the first step toward entering the full-time Christian ministry. Further steps entail college training and, if possible, theological training also. Assuming that all such necessary training has been completed, in due time the young local preacher comes back before the District Committee on Ministerial Qualifications asking for a recommendation to the Annual Conference for "admission on trial."

Traveling Preachers

At the next session of his Annual Conference the candidate for admission, having secured the recommendation of his district committee, appears before the Annual Conference's Board of Ministerial Training and Qualifications. That board is composed of men who are members of the Annual Conference. They examine him much more carefully as to his education, his fitness for the ministry, his Christian intent and experience, and his gifts and abilities. If he satisfies the group that he is well qualified to be a Christian minister, the board recommends him to the Annual Conference in open session for admission. The conference thereupon votes to admit him "on trial." This starts him as a *traveling preacher* under appointment by the bishop.

The usual conference novitiate remains on trial for two years. This period gives the conference an opportunity to observe the man's work, since he is at once put in charge of a pastorate. If the person on trial gives evidence of fitness for and success in the ministry, at the end of his second year the conference votes to admit him into "full connection."

That means that the man is to be received into full conference membership. This is done in a formal and solemn manner by the bishop, who asks him, and possibly others who are to be received, certain soul-searching questions in the presence of the entire conference. The questions to be answered were provided by John Wesley himself, in order to test and put on record those who were to be admitted to the Methodist preacherhood. They have been asked of every preacher from Wesley's day to ours and serve to make the candidate declare publicly his personal Christian faith and ministerial intent. This having been done and the bishop's examination concluded to the satisfaction of the conference, the bishop puts the name to a vote and formally receives the man—or usually a class or group of men—into the conference. This puts him into the regular traveling ministry of the entire Methodist Church.

Ordination

The Methodist Church confers upon its ministers a special status in providing that each under certain carefully outlined procedures may be ordained to one or to both of the two "orders" of the Christian ministry in which Methodists believe. These are the order of DEACONS and the order of ELDERS.

Deacons

The office of deacon is the lower of Methodism's two orders. It is an ancient one, coming down from the time of the Apostles. Stephen was a deacon, one of the first seven (Acts 6:5), and was a powerful preacher, being full of the Holy Ghost. He was ordained deacon by the Apostles. Philip was another deacon and preacher. "Then Philip went down to the city of Samaria, and preached Christ unto them." (Acts 8:5.) Philip expounded the Scriptures to the Ethiopian eunuch and administered to him the rite of baptism.

Deacons were clearly ministers in the early Church and are so in Methodism. A deacon today can (within his own charge) perform all the ministerial practices of the church. He cannot, however, administer the sacrament of Holy Communion *outside the bounds of his own charge*, though he can assist an ordained elder whenever requested.

Baptists and Presbyterians hold the deacon to be a layman set apart to look after the temporal affairs of the local church (similar to our steward). Most Methodists, however, agree with Bishop John Emory that the "Scriptural evidence for the order of deacons, as an order of ministers distinct from that of elders or bishops, is too plain to be thus lightly treated."

To become a deacon, the Annual Conference must elect a man to "deacons' orders." This having been done, the bishop in a formal rite or ceremony lays his hands upon the head of the man to be ordained and pronounces him a deacon in the Church of God. This gives the man permanent ministerial rights. He may preach the gospel, bury the dead, marry people where the laws of his state permit, conduct the rite of baptism, and assist in the administration of the sacrament of Holy Communion.

Elders

The highest ministerial order in Methodism is that of elder. The word "elder" is the translation of the Greek *presbyteros* or the Latin *presbyter,* from which came the word "priest" in English. John Wesley did not like the title "priest" (the name the Church of England yet keeps for this order of ministers) and changed it to "elder." Methodism has kept the name ever since.

A minister who is a deacon may be elected to the order of elders by an Annual Conference. This must also be by formal vote.

The ordination of elders is a much more elaborate ceremony than that of deacons. In this ceremony other elders join with the bishop in placing their hands upon the head of the person to be ordained, while the bishop prays that he may be imbued with the Holy Spirit "for the office and work of an elder in the Church of God."

An ordained elder has all the rights and privileges of the Christian ministry in The Methodist Church. Chief among these is the permanent right to administer the sacraments. Until very recently no one not ordained as an elder ever could administer the sacrament. However, at late General Conferences the right to administer the sacraments has been given to deacons and even to local preachers regularly appointed as preachers in charge, provided that they do this *only within the bounds of their own charge.* An ordained elder, however, is empowered to administer the sacraments anywhere.

A man may be ordained as deacon or elder in The Methodist Church under certain carefully observed provisions even though he may not be a member of an Annual Conference. So local preachers may qualify to be ordained as elders and have the right to administer the Communion as "local elders." Likewise men who have been in the Annual Conference as regular traveling elders may be "located," that is, leave the traveling ministry and become local preachers again without forfeiting their rights as deacons or elders as the case may be.

Pastors

A PASTOR—officially known as a "preacher in charge"—is one who has been appointed to a church or circuit as its regular minister. The duties of a pastor are:

1. To preach the gospel.

2. To administer the sacraments, perform marriage ceremonies, and bury the dead.

3. To visit from house to house, so as to give guidance and oversight to church members and to others in need of a pastor's help.

4. To instruct candidates for membership in the church and to receive members and dismiss them when they move to other locations.

5. To form classes of children and adults in preparation for church membership and to train them for living a Christian life.

6. To have general charge of the worship of the church in its various ways; to have oversight of other preachers in the pastoral charge; to organize and maintain church schools, Woman's Societies of Christian Service, young people's organizations, organizations of Methodist Men; to see that all the provisions of the *Discipline* are maintained in the pastoral charge and that the ordinances and regulations of the church are duly observed.

Twenty-seven specific duties are outlined for the pastor in the 1952 *Discipline*—some in general terms but all making the pastoral office the most important in the whole connection. The pastor is the key man, and the progress of each local church, both spiritually and temporally, depends on the one who serves it as preacher in charge.

District Superintendents

The DISTRICT SUPERINTENDENT is a most important administrative officer in The Methodist Church. The bishop in charge of an Annual Conference, in making up his appointments, must select a certain number of men and appoint them to be district superintendents. To each of these is entrusted the supervision of the churches within a geographic area, or district.

The chief duty of a district superintendent is to travel through his district continually, in order to preach and to oversee the temporal and spiritual affairs of all the churches. He has general charge of all the traveling and local preachers in his district; and he may change, receive, or appoint preachers during intervals between conferences in the absence of the bishop.

The district superintendent does much of his work through the Quarterly Conferences, which he must hold in each one of his charges at stated intervals during the year. He is a pastor of pastors; he is a member of the "bishop's cabinet" and thus has a direct part in the making of appointments; he is expected to see that the program of the church, as outlined by the *Discipline*, is carried out within his district; and he must represent the preachers of his district before the bishop and the other members of the cabinet in all matters having to do with appointments.

Laymen often fail to realize the importance of the district superintendency in Methodism. They only see the district superintendent perhaps at two of the Quarterly Conferences during the year and thus do not have full appreciation of the work he does. To a far greater degree than is realized, the whole Methodist connection functions through the district superintendent. His work, while not always manifest nor spectacular, is felt throughout every department of church and conference work.

Bishops

The BISHOP in Methodist polity is the highest officer of the church and the executive and general administrator of the church's work and program in the Annual Conferences assigned to him. Bishops are elected by the Jurisdictional Conferences and are *consecrated*, not ordained.

In the Protestant Episcopal Church bishops are regarded as belonging to a third order. That church has deacons, elders ("priests," they are called), and bishops. In Methodism, as has been explained, there are only two orders, deacons and elders; the bishop is simply an elder who is set apart for a peculiar administrative task—that of a superintendent in the church.

The principal duties of a bishop are:

1. To oversee the spiritual and temporal affairs of the Church.

2. To preside over the General, Jurisdictional, Central, and Annual Conferences.

3. To fix the appointments of the preachers.

4. To form the districts within each Annual Conference.

5. To ordain elders and deacons after he is authorized to do so.

6. To travel through the connection at large.

Of these duties the most important is that of stationing the preachers. This heavy responsibility is, however, shared by the cabinet of district superintendents, each of whom is largely responsible for the appointments made within his district. But the bishop has the final word, and Methodism holds him responsible for the way his area is manned and administered.

Stewards

STEWARDS and trustees are lay officers of the local church. Stewards are elected annually by the Quarterly Conference at the session next preceding a meeting of the Annual Conference.

A steward must be not less than eighteen years of age and must be nominated by the committee on nominations of the Quarterly Conference. Of this committee the pastor is chairman. Where there is no committee on nominations, the pastor himself nominates.

Stewards are required to be "persons of genuine Christian character who love the church and are competent to administer its affairs." Stewards really compose the pastor's "cabinet," and it is for this reason that the *Discipline* gives the pastor chief responsibility in nominating them. Wise pastors see that the best men and women are named for the position, taking into consideration the different elements and varying talents represented in the local church.

Stewards must be elected, or re-elected, annually. Each steward takes his office at the beginning of the new conference year following his election. If a steward is elected to fill a vacancy, he takes office immediately.

The duties of a steward are:

1. To serve as a member of the Quarterly Conference, attend its meetings, and act on its committees and commissions.

2. To serve as a member of the Official Board, attend its meetings, and serve on its committees.

3. To set an example to the congregation by attendance at church, liberality in giving, and loyalty to Methodist doctrine and discipline.

4. To counsel with the pastor concerning the affairs of the church. In former days the *Discipline* stated that a prime duty of stewards was "to tell the preacher what they think is wrong in him." Good stewards then, and now, can advise their pastor tactfully and helpfully.

Stewards traditionally have been responsible for the finances of the local church; their voice in the Quarterly Conference determines:

1. What the charge shall pay as salary to the minister or ministers.

2. What shall be the "acceptance" on the part of the local church —that is, what the charge shall raise—on the general funds of the church. They have the right to accept, reject, or modify the allotment apportioned their church as its share of general or conference funds.

3. What shall be the amount to be raised for other purposes in the local church and how this shall be expended.

In raising the necessary funds for the church and its work, everything depends on the energetic and effective work of the stewards. No other members of the church feel free to act in their places. Stewards therefore should do their work well or resign promptly. *"Faithfulness* in this office," says H. T. Hudson, "is of the highest importance to the welfare of the ministry and the prosperity of the Church." [1]

Besides these financial duties the stewards in the Official Board and Quarterly Conference have great authority in managing and directing all affairs of the local church. Through

[1] *Op. cit.*

the four commissions set up by the Quarterly Conference (Membership and Evangelism, Education, Missions, and Finance) the whole range of the church's interests are directed and supervised. While the financial responsibility usually gives the most concern to church officials, all other temporal interests of their church are to be supervised by them also.

John Wesley created the office of steward and chose the name for it. He found it necessary to select certain trusted men in each of his Methodist societies to look after the contributions of the group and take care of temporal welfare. The office grew in effectiveness and influence as the years went by, and today a layman can have no higher honor nor greater responsibility than to be chosen by his pastor and fellow church members to be a steward in the church. The whole temporal economy of Methodism rests on the shoulders of these men and women. Generously and unselfishly through the length and breadth of Methodism they are serving in every local church as co-workers with their pastor and with one another in doing the work of God.

Trustees

TRUSTEES are officials of the local church who have been duly elected to manage the church property. They hold it in trust, not for the local congregation, but for The Methodist Church.

Each local church must have a Board of Trustees, consisting of not fewer than three nor more than nine persons. Each must be over twenty-one years of age, and at least two thirds of them must be members of The Methodist Church.

Trustees are elected by the Quarterly Conference, each for a term of three years; the elections are so arranged that only one third of each Board of Trustees need be elected in any one year. Trustees are nominated by the committee on nominations of the Quarterly Conference, and of this committee the pastor is of course, always chairman.

The great duty of the trustees is to hold and manage the church property as directed by the Quarterly Conference. All matters affecting the buying, selling, or mortgaging of the church property are handled through them. They are expected to report carefully once a year regarding their work and responsibility. Persons of sound judgment and of substance and repute in the community usually are chosen as trustees. The duties of this office are not onerous, but they are important, and it is an honor to be a trustee of The Methodist Church.

The Itinerancy

A marked feature of Methodism is the itinerancy of its ministry, that is, the plan of moving ministers from one field of work to another. The itinerant system requires three things:

1. That the congregations give up their right to choose their ministers.

2. That the preachers give up their right to select their own fields of labor.

3. That the appointment be made by a competent, impartial, untrammeled authority (the bishop), whose powers and duties must be outlined carefully and ordered by the whole church.

As the surrender of these rights on the part of the local churches and the preachers is a very real one, it required years of tension, as well as great unselfishness, to establish itinerancy during the formative period of Methodism. But once having been established, it has justified itself in unmistakable ways.

Our plan of itinerancy is based upon the world-parish conception of Methodism. A preacher in one place must be ready to be a preacher in all places. "Go ye into all the world, and preach the gospel to every creature" has been a command that Methodism has taken seriously. "Go ye"— not "wait until the people come to you." In a settled, non-traveling ministry the people *call* the preacher; he can accept or reject each call. But in the itinerant system the appointive power tells each preacher what is to be his church and tells each church who is to be its preacher. This is done for an entire Annual Conference of traveling preachers once a year when the appointments are read.

It is not commonly understood even among Methodists that the appointments *must all be made together* and, therefore, that each depends on the others. Each preacher and each church naturally is interested most of all in his own particular assignment. But every particular appointment is locked in a tight unity with every other appointment, since no preacher can be left without a charge and no charge without a preacher. It is easy enough for a church committee on "pastoral relations" to tell the bishop and district superintendent which man they want, or do not want, for their preacher. But no one church's wishes can be carried out without affecting the wishes of every other church and minister in the conference. Any undue insistence on the part of a local church, or on that of a minister, to get special wishes carried out in the making of the appointments may break in upon and badly injure the work of other churches or ministers, if such wishes are allowed. This is something which loyal Methodists should always realize.

Great responsibility rests on the bishop and his cabinet to see that no selfish pressure from any one church, nor from any one minister, no matter how influential, shall keep them from making the very best slate of appointments that can be made. Every good bishop keeps in mind the "care of all the churches," as the apostle Paul expressed it.

The advantages of the itinerant system are:

1. Every preacher gets a place, and every place gets a preacher. Weak churches, as well as strong ones, are always supplied with ministers.

2. There are no leftover preachers and no vacant churches in Methodism—no unemployed preachers waiting for some church to call them nor any period of waiting between appointments. Local preachers, as has been explained, are not members of the Annual Conference and make their living in some secular way, preaching when they can. But the regular traveling ministry of Methodism is composed of men each of whom has a job and is expected to be at work at it.

3. The itinerancy furnishes the people with a variety of ministerial talent and puts each minister on his mettle to lead and serve churches of various types as he continues to travel. The itinerant system is the foe of lethargy, and a succession of different ministers in each church prevents the desuetude that may attend the long pastorate of one man, who may feel tempted to settle down into a ministerial routine.

4. It makes for a wise church strategy and for an efficient manning of all charges, since it gives the appointive power a chance to fill to best advantage every church in the conference. Where a congregation needs a seasoned minister to offset what may have been a former unwise, overenthusiastic, pastoral leadership; or where a young minister may be needed to supply a church which has been too long under an elderly preacher; where a church has burned down and they need a "builder," or a new church has been built and they need a "debt payer," or a preacher is called for to "fill the pews," or a pastor to gather the flock closer together—then the

itinerant system gives the bishop and cabinet a chance to pick the very best man for each special place.

5. It guarantees each minister a pulpit for his lifetime. In the churches which call their ministers this is not the case. A man may find himself out of a pulpit in middle life, sometimes through situations over which he has no control. And since churches want younger men who may be expected to give them a long-term ministry, the displaced minister past middle life may not receive any acceptable calls. To be sure, no man in the itinerant system, when he comes to his waning years, will be able to command as large a church as when he was at the height of his powers—nor should he. But Methodism finds a place for the minister who must decrease as well as for the young man who is growing in ministerial life.

6. Pastoral changes and adjustments can be more easily made under the itinerant system than under any other. Where a minister does not fit, the embarrassment of requesting his resignation or of voting him out, as would be necessary in congregationally governed churches, does not occur. The appointive power in Methodism is simply apprised of the situation, and at the next conference the man can be moved quietly and another minister put in his place. The violence and strife frequently attending pastoral changes in other connections are thus usually avoided. Sometimes the minister rather than his people desires a change, and he has the right to suggest to the district superintendent that he be moved to another place.

7. While both people and preachers give up their rights in the actual making of the appointments, they enjoy the following important safeguards against any arbitrary or ill-considered exercise of the appointive power:

a) Each church has a Committee on Pastoral Relations,

which must co-operate with the pastor, the district superintendent, and the bishop in arranging for a change of pastors. This committee is amenable to the Quarterly Conference and is expected to represent the wishes of the local church. The committee must speak as the Quarterly Conference directs it to do, regarding any move or possible move, any minister or possible minister who may be requested as pastor. The Committee on Pastoral Relations is therefore not an independent agency, though a Quarterly Conference may empower the committee to use its own best judgment in the matter of arranging for a change of pastors. This committee, of course, is advisory only, since the bishop has the final word, but its wishes are heard with great respect by the appointive power.

Since the *Discipline* of the church provides for an official Committee on Pastoral Relations in every local church, it is expected that the wishes and desires of the local church will be expressed through that committee. Unofficial requests, private letters to the bishop, and anonymous complaints concerning the pastor are disregarded by the bishop and his cabinet, who very properly look to the powerful Committee on Pastoral Relations to guide them as to what the congregation wants.

b) Each pastor must be consulted by his district superintendent before a final announcement of the appointment shall be made. Usually any contemplated move affecting a minister is discussed with him well in advance of the Annual Conference. This gives him an opportunity to express his wishes and give his judgment upon the proposed appointment.

c) The bishop must be guided by the members of his cabinet—the district superintendents—in the making of each and all appointments. The case of every minister and every church is represented by the district superintendent in whose district the man or the church happens to be. No bishop is allowed to make any appointment by private, secret fiat. He must read the entire list of appointments to the entire cabinet before he makes the appointments official by reading them to the Annual Conference.

d) Practically, under the appointive system both people and preachers get their wishes carried out as quickly—sometimes more quickly—than under the "call" system. It is a truism that in the long run every preacher makes his own appointment; each church gets the sort of preacher its size and enthusiasm warrant.

Commenting on the itinerant system, a robust Methodist authority of some years ago said, "We believe the plan to be providential; it has worked wonders, and we expect to adhere to it till the trump of judgment sounds." [2]

---

[2] *Ibid.*

CHAPTER SEVEN

Worship and the Sacraments

METHODISTS worship as do other Christians—publicly and privately. The General Rules of our church insist that everyone should "attend upon the public worship of God, the ministry of the Word, the Supper of the Lord, and family and private prayer."

Methodist public worship has always been of two types. It is "free" in the usual services of the church; but it is liturgical, or ordered, in the stated ceremonies called for by our ritual.

We are free in the sense that we are not bound to any special form or order of worship. We can pray or sing or preach or read scripture at any time, just as may seem fitting to the worshiping congregation or its leader. Early Methodists had a reputation for being completely untrammeled in worship, their spontaneity and enthusiasm being in strong contrast to the stiffness of the Prayer Book and its ordered ceremoniousness. But when we engage in the recurrent rites of the church, such as Communion, baptism, marriage, funerals, ordinations, and so on, Methodism has always strictly followed a time-honored ritual.

For many years Methodist worship revolved entirely around the sermon. Readings, prayers, and the like were as varied as the congregations that participated in them. After a time the church began to drop into a regular pattern of worship and at length worked out what we now call our "orders of worship." These are published in the Hymnal, in the book of *Discipline,* and in the *Book of Worship.*

Many Methodists insist that since the Church provides orders of worship, they should be followed in all places without any variation. But others say that printed orders are suggestive only and in the name of Christian liberty feel free to vary them.

The Orders of Worship

"In recognition of the various needs of our several congregations," the *Discipline* says, "four orders of worship have been provided which may be used according to desire."

Each of these orders outlines a program of hymns, prayers, readings, and, of course, the sermon. Every congregation is free to modify any chosen order to fit local custom or desire.

Order of Worship I is a well-rounded program for formal Sunday-morning worship.

Order of Worship II is a slightly less formal program and is considered most suitable for evening worship.

Order of Worship III differs very little from Order II.

Order of Worship IV is an "Order for Morning or Evening Prayer, Adapted from the Sunday Service of John Wesley" and "Suggested for Occasional Use." This is an elaborate form, since it is a repetition of the same office in the English *Book of Common Prayer.* It is very seldom used.

THE HYMNAL AND SINGING

Prominent in every order of worship are the hymns. Methodists have ever been a singing people. *The Methodist Hymnal* is one of the great hymnbooks of the world and contains among its 644 hymns a rich wealth of devotional material both in words and in music. These hymns cover every aspect of Christian life. There are seasonal hymns, such as those for Christmas, Thanksgiving, Easter, and patriotic occasions; there are devotional hymns, penitential hymns, exultant hymns; there are hymns of aspiration and praise; hymns for children, hymns for youth, hymns of social welfare, hymns of the past and hymns of the present. Happy the people whose minister is able to develop in them an appreciation of and a love for the hymns made available to them in our *Methodist Hymnal*.

THE READING OF THE SCRIPTURES

This is a necessary and edifying part of our public worship. Formerly it was done entirely by the minister. Now, however, the participation of the congregation in the public reading of the Word is called for through the use of responsive readings found in the Hymnal. These readings have been carefully chosen, and apply to all the experiences of the Christian life and cover the various seasons of the Christian year. The reading of the scripture by the minister is done from the pulpit or lectern. Many ministers like to expound as they read, taking a moment or two to explain the context or the special meaning of a particular passage. The Bible, all agree, should always be read reverently and impressively. A substantial lesson, not simply a few verses, most ministers feel, should be chosen on each occasion.

PUBLIC PRAYER

Public prayer is by its nature at the heart of all Christian worship. There are Christian groups who do not believe in singing, there are those who do not believe in the public reading of the Word, but all religious people believe in prayer. The minister is expected to lead the people in public prayer; and the "pastoral," or "general prayer," called for in our orders of worship, is a special feature of that worship which ought never to be neglected. There are ministers who put as much time on the preparation of their public prayers as they do upon the sermon itself. In a true pastoral prayer the minister is praying *for* and *on behalf of* the people, not simply out of some immediate personal feelings of his own.

The *Book of Worship,* compiled by an official Commission on Worship and adopted by the General Conference for optional use among Methodists, contains a well-arranged collection of prayers for both public and private use. This book should be in the homes of our people, for in it can be found a veritable treasury of prayers and acts of devotion.

THE SERMON

The sermon has, of course, been the prime feature of Methodist congregational gatherings since the time of Wesley. We are a preaching church; and while we have been mighty in singing and, we trust, fervent in prayer, yet through the preaching of the Word, Methodism seems to have borne its greatest witness.

It is not proper, however, to regard the sermon alone as the "service" for everything from the first sound of the organ's voluntary until the final benediction is a part of one unified offering of praise to God.

Other features of Methodist worship, such as the call to worship, offertory, announcements, final prayers, and benediction, likewise have a part in a richly rounded service. The order of worship which each local church adopts for its own should become familiar to every worshiper so that each person may participate as fully as possible.

Beside the regular orders of worship, provision is made for less formal occasions when Christian people are encouraged to assemble for prayer or praise, for watch night or prayer meeting, for thanksgiving or for comradeship. Evening worship is less formal than that for morning, and evangelistic services are traditionally even more free. Each kind of service has a value in its own way. Reverence and a due regard for the decency and order which should always prevail among Christian people will be the guide, even where printed forms are not provided.

Methodists go to church as their Christian privilege, being assured that in so doing they will receive a blessing if they bring to the service a proper mind and an open heart. It is not possible to have great preachers in each pulpit. Indeed, with all Methodism's emphasis on preaching, we have never had in every one of our pulpits men attractive in speech and bearing. But we have had, and now have, sincere, earnest expounders of God's Word, men who have been called and consecrated to the Christian ministry; and these men are endeavoring to give their best from the pulpit Sunday by Sunday. Our people will always find under the ministry of such men spiritual sustenance and help. Every loyal Methodist should and is privileged to go to church and take his place.

The Ritual

The Methodist ritual embodies the fixed forms of worship for Communion, baptism, burial, marriage, reception of church members, the ordaining of ministers, and the like. While there is value in varying the program of worship in the usual Sunday service, regularity in conducting the stated rites of the church is demanded by our *Discipline*. "Let our ritual be invariably used," was the old injunction. "A decent ritual," observed Bishop Holland McTyeire, "is the best guard against formality."

John Wesley gave to Methodism the rites and ceremonies which are in our ritual. He took these from the prayer book of the Church of England and revised them slightly. This will explain the likeness of our Communion service, our marriage and burial services, to those of the Protestant Episcopal Church, since both the Methodists and Episcopalians took these forms from the same English prayer book. Methodists, however, do not "use the Episcopal service" any more than the Episcopalians "use" the Methodist service. Both follow what has sometimes been called the "English Rite."

It will not be possible to outline even in the briefest way all the separate offices in the Methodist ritual. There is one, however—the sacrament of the Lord's Supper—which is so important as the great ordinance and recurrent rite of the Church that the method of its observance should be carefully outlined. Every Methodist should understand the meaning of the separate readings, prayers, and devotional acts he is summoned to engage in at each celebration of the Lord's Supper.

The Order for the Administration of the Sacrament of the Lord's Supper or Holy Communion

The Lord's Supper is perhaps the most sacred service of the Christian Church. Christians everywhere observe it in memory of Christ, who instituted and commanded it. The way the Lord's Supper is observed varies among different groups of Christians, but all celebrate it with the utmost reverence.

Methodists hold that the Communion of the Lord's Supper is a means of grace and a sign and symbol of the redemptive work of Christ, our Lord. It is both a memorial and a living experience. It is a *memorial* in that through it we remember Christ and the sacrifice he made for us; it is a *living experience* in that each person who reverently engages in it can find it to be an immediate experience of comfort and blessing.

Our *Discipline* commands us to observe the Communion at stated intervals, and no Christian church can fail to celebrate it with regularity. Methodist churches usually observe it either monthly or quarterly.

Who may administer the Communion? Regular, ordained ministers of our own or sister evangelical churches are competent to celebrate the Lord's Supper. In Methodist practice an elder (a minister who has been fully ordained) must always be in charge of a service of Holy Communion. However, if a minister who is not an elder has been appointed to have charge of a special church, he may conduct the Communion service within the precincts of his own church—as has been before explained.

Methodists may feel free to take the Communion at the hands of any consecrated minister of any other Christian church when they are invited to do so.

Who may communicate? [1] Every member of The Methodist Church who is in good standing is expected to take Communion when it is made available. The invitation, which is read as a formal part of the ritual, invites those who "truly and earnestly repent of [their] sins, and are in love and charity with [their] neighbors, and intend to lead a new life," to "draw near with faith." Members of other Christian denominations are cordially invited to join with us at the Communion table.

Children of the church who have not yet been admitted to church membership are not usually at the Communion table. There is no fixed rule forbidding them to come, however, and children sometimes come forward with other members of the

[1] "Communicate" is the technical name for receiving Communion. We often shorten it to "commune."

family. However, as the Communion is considered a privilege of duly admitted church members, children are not encouraged to communicate until they have reached the age of discretion, when they should become members of the church in their own right and so take their places about the table.

Our church provides two orders for conducting the Lord's Supper: Order I, which was in use in the former Methodist Episcopal Church; and Order II, that of the former Methodist Episcopal Church, South. These orders are very much alike as each represents only a slight revision of the original Methodist Communion service.

The main features of the Methodist sacramental service are set forth below. It is a beautifully balanced rite in which the first prayers and readings are designed to prepare the worshiper for the reception of Communion itself.

Long-continued custom calls for the Lord's table to have upon it a "fair linen cloth," which covers the "elements," as the bread and wine are termed. The pure, unfermented juice of the grape is the symbolic wine called for by our ritual. Methodist regulations have long forbidden the use of regular wine.

Methodists come forward and kneel when they receive the Communion, but our church allows persons who have scruples against kneeling to receive the elements either seated or standing. In early days a great many Protestants felt that kneeling at the Communion table was too suggestive of the Roman Catholic practice of worshiping the Host, as is done in the Mass. But today such scruples are of little weight, and no one who comes to a Methodist Communion table objects to kneeling.

The Communion service proper begins when the minister,

standing by the Lord's Table, makes preparation to receive the offering for the needy.[2]

OFFERING FOR THE NEEDY

The collection for the poor at the time of Communion is a very ancient Christian practice. The money received through this special offering is a sacred trust and is administered through the poor fund of the local church.

THE OFFERTORY SENTENCES

("Let your light so shine before men," and so on.) These offertory sentences are read during the taking of this offering or as a prelude to it. Three or four of these brief sentences are usually read, even where the custom prevails of having the communicants lay their offering within the chancel rail when they come forward to commune. After the offering has been taken, comes the invitation.

THE INVITATION

This begins with the majestic "Ye that do truly and earnestly repent of your sins, and are in love and charity with your neighbors, and intend to lead a new life, . . . draw near with faith. . . ."

Following this the minister and people, kneeling, read together as a prayer the general confession.

THE GENERAL CONFESSION

("Almighty God, Father of our Lord Jesus Christ, Maker of all things. . . .") This ancient expression of Christian penitence and plea for mercy has come down to us from the

[2] It is suggested that the reader open his Hymnal or *Discipline* to the Communion office and follow carefully the analysis and explanation of the several parts of it as they are given here.

first Prayer Book of 1549 almost unchanged. Read in unison by all, it serves to unite the worshiping congregation in a cry of confession and call for forgiveness.

THE ABSOLUTION

The absolution, as it was formerly called, is next. ("Almighty God, our heavenly Father, who of thy great mercy. . . .") It is read by the minister and is designed to follow the plea for forgiveness—just made in the General Confession —with the assurance that since God has "promised forgiveness of sins to all them that with hearty repentance and true faith" turn unto him, he will "have mercy upon us; pardon and deliver us from all our sins; confirm and strengthen us in all goodness; and bring us to everlasting life."

THE COMFORTABLE WORDS

These are read next by the minister. ("If any man sin, we have an advocate with the Father. . . .") These four sentences are designed to give the worshiper a further assurance of comfort, pardon, and peace.

THE SURSUM CORDA

The mood of the service now suddenly changes. Up to this point there has been a confession of sin and a plea for forgiveness, followed by gentle, comforting words, as the people are prepared more definitely for the reception of Communion. But now the minister suddenly says: "Lift up your hearts."

PEOPLE: "We lift them up unto the Lord."
MINISTER: "Let us give thanks unto the Lord."
PEOPLE: "It is meet and right so to do."

The note is of strong, robust thankfulness, and immediately after there follows the exultant Trisagion.

TRISAGION

"Thrice holy"—the passage from Isaiah. "Therefore with angels and archangels, and with all the company of heaven, ... evermore praising thee, and saying: Holy, holy, holy. . . ."

The exultant note now struck brings to the worshiper a feeling of the glory and power of God.

THE PRAYER OF HUMBLE ACCESS

This prayer has traditionally come next. ("We do not presume to come to this thy table.") It precedes the Prayer of Consecration in the English prayer book and in our Order II. It is a beautiful expression, pleading the right to come to the Communion table not "trusting in our own righteousness, but in thy manifold and great mercies."

THE PRAYER OF CONSECRATION

("Almighty God, our heavenly Father, who of thy tender mercy didst give thine only Son Jesus Christ to suffer death upon the cross for our redemption. . . .") This prayer is the focus of the pre-Communion service. Every word of it has been fought over through the ages in an endeavor to make it a true expression of the Christian faith and at the same time to consecrate the elements of the Lord's Supper. It is remembered that the Lord himself blessed the original elements (Matt. 26:26), and Paul speaks of the "cup of blessing which we bless" (I Cor. 10:16). The present prayer does not fix its petition on the *elements,* but on the *communicants*— "that *we,* receiving this bread and wine, according to thy Son our Saviour Jesus Christ's holy institution, . . . may also be partakers of the divine nature through him."

Following comes the actual communication of the minister.

COMMUNICATION OF THE MINISTER

The minister, or ministers, take the Communion first, not in order to show any superiority over the people, but better to manage and control the service—"that they may be readye to helpe the chiefe Minister," the old prayer book used to say.

Receiving the Communion "in both kinds" means both bread and wine. Our church, with all Protestantism, wants to make it explicit that there shall be no denial of the cup to the laity. Both elements are taken at each Communion.

THE COMMUNICATION OF THE PEOPLE

By long-continued custom the people come forward and kneel about the chancel rail when the Communion is received. This is a practice which is to be continued wherever possible. In the interest of time the custom has grown within some churches of passing the elements through the pews where the congregation is seated. But much is lost if the individual worshiper cannot move forward and thus in a public way and by his own act "proclaim Christ's death until his coming again." Each communicant's participation becomes a part of the general witness.

After the people have finished communing, the ministers are directed to place upon the Lord's table what remains of the consecrated elements and cover them with the linen cloth again. Then comes a great prayer in which both minister and people join.

THE PRAYER OF THANKSGIVING

It is a matchless petition ("O Lord, our heavenly Father, we, thy humble servants, desire thy fatherly goodness mercifully to accept this our sacrifice of praise and thanksgiving. . . .") Like other parts of this office it is a very old prayer, written by Thomas Cranmer at the time of the Reformation.

146

It ends with a petition that God shall accept our offering of ourselves, "not weighing our merits, but pardoning our offenses; through Jesus Christ our Lord."

THE GLORIA IN EXCELSIS

("Glory be to God on high, and on earth peace, good will toward men. . . .") The people are directed to stand for this prayer, which is addressed to Christ as Lord. It is the only prayer in the ritual made directly to Christ, the "Lamb of God . . . that takest away the sins of the world." The alliterative effect of the final petitions of this prayer and the plea that Christ shall have mercy upon his worshipers make the prayer one of the most moving in the entire book.

THE BENEDICTION

The minister pronounces the benediction as the people continue in the attitude of prayer.

Private Communion and Communion in the home are often arranged for the benefit of those who are sick. Here the service is usually much simpler, though the Prayer of Consecration is always to be read. Good ministers know how to adapt this service to the spiritual needs of those to whom they are ministering.

Baptism

Baptism is the other Sacrament of the Christian Church. It differs from the Lord's Supper in that while the latter is repeated frequently for people in the full maturity of their Christian lives, Baptism is celebrated once and for all in each individual life.

Baptism has always been the gateway to the Christian Church. It was so in the early days, and the New Testament

147

gives incident after incident where becoming baptized was equivalent to assuming the pledge of Christian discipleship.

At a very early date children were brought into the Church through baptism. Later on it was felt that when children grew to the age of accountability, they should speak for themselves with relation to church membership. So the office of Confirmation was begun in the ancient Church and is continued today in the Roman Catholic Church, the Church of England, and the Protestant Episcopal Church. Methodism, however, has never had a confirmation service as such, though we do have a Form for the Reception of Members very similar to it.

Infant Baptism

Methodists together with the great majority of Christians believe strongly in the baptism of infants. Through this act parents dedicate their children to Almighty God, and the church believes that God uses baptism to claim his own and put his seal upon them in a unique way. One authority referred to infant baptism as "matriculation in the school of Christ." "To christen" is the same as "to baptize."

Those who oppose infant baptism do so on the ground that since an unknowing infant can have no awareness of the act of baptism done on his behalf, the rite therefore is meaningless. But overwhelming is the testimony of the Christian ages in which from the earliest days infant baptism has been practiced. Had infant baptism been something which was begun *after* apostolic times, it would have created a revolution in the Church—and of such we do not find the slightest sign. On the contrary we read in the Acts of the Apostles how three thousand were baptized on the day of Pentecost (Acts 2:41); and that five households were baptized at other times (Acts 10:48; 16:15, 33; I Cor. 1:16; 16:15). This could scarcely have been possible unless children were included, especially when we remember that Peter preached on the day of Pentecost that the "promise is unto you, and to your children."

Prior to a service of infant baptism the minister is required to talk with the parents concerning the meaning of the baptismal sacrament and the obligation they will be expected to assume, promising to bring up their child in the Christian faith.

Baptism in the home is allowable and is often practiced, but its celebration in the church is much to be preferred. This gives an opportunity for the congregation, representing the Christian brotherhood, to participate in the service. Also since baptism is the gateway of the church, it is symbolically fitting that the rite take place in the church sanctuary itself.

Methodism has never put much stress on the idea of having sponsors, or godparents, at a baptismal service. The Church of England and the Protestant Episcopal Church provide for sponsors, the idea being that there should be persons who are not physically kin to the infant who will act as "godkin," or spiritual parents. John Wesley, when he edited the baptismal office for American Methodism, left out the regulation calling for sponsors and made no reference to them.

In Methodist practice parents are held responsible for presenting their children for baptism and are the ones who are expected to respond. There would be no objection to godparents in a Methodist baptismal service, and indeed our ritual now refers to "parents or sponsors." But the emphasis with us is upon the great duty of the parents, and *they take the vows for themselves* and not for the child.

The Rite of Baptism

This is carefully outlined in the ritual. The entire office is one that calls for dignity and unhurried celebration of this

Sacrament of Christ. Those who abridge it in the presence of a waiting congregation so that "time may be saved" may make it a perfunctory and hasty ceremony devoid of that solemnity which should accompany one of the sacred acts of life.

Mode of Baptism

There has been a long controversy in church history over the mode of baptism. In American life this was provoked by Baptists and other aggressive evangelical communions who affirmed that no baptism could be valid unless the body of the believer had been totally immersed in water. Methodism, with most other Christian bodies, denies this, holding that while immersion is one valid mode, so are sprinkling and pouring equally valid modes.

It is the custom in our church to sprinkle water upon the person being baptized. But if an adult is extremely desirous of being baptized by immersion, our ministers are instructed to let him have his wish.

The appeal to the Scriptures by those who favor immersion in order to determine New Testament practice has always been met with a counter appeal, and no sound New Testament scholar has ever been able to be sure regarding apostolic practice. Methodists believe that the weight of evidence is in favor of pouring or sprinkling.

Those who support immersion build their argument upon the statement that Christ went to the Jordan to be baptized of John, and so he did. But it is not certain that immersion was the method used. The essential matter in ceremonial washing was that the water should be "living," that is, running water. The Jordan provided living water as did any spring.

Even admitting for the sake of argument that the whole apostolic Church used immersion as its method of baptism (which surely cannot be proved), the living Church of the present would not necessarily feel bound by this mode any more than the fact that the apostles reclined on the floor when they partook of the Last Supper would force us to do likewise today at our Communion services. Symbolism underlies the whole rite, and Christians must be tolerant of one another's practices. If anyone wishes to be immersed, let him be immersed; but let him not deny the validity of the baptism of others who use another mode.

The Baptism of Adults

The service for the baptism of adults is much like that for infants in its general plan of readings, prayers, and so on. The distinctive feature of the adult service, however, is that the person being baptized assumes the vows *by personal response*. No sponsor has ever been thought of in connection with this office.

The vows which are taken during this rite are quite definitive in outlining a person's will and intent. The ancient baptismal vow was a triple one—of "repentance, faith, and obedience." Rather elaborate questions were asked of the convert in former days. Now the minister combines the questions so as to ask for an acceptance of Christ and "an earnest endeavor to keep God's holy will and commandments."

A person must be baptized before he can be formally received into The Methodist Church. When, therefore, an adult who never has been baptized before is to be received into the Church, it is a common practice on the part of the ministers to combine the service of Adult Baptism with that for the Reception of Members. In such cases the baptism is followed immediately with one further question to the convert. This asks him to certify loyalty to The Methodist Church, and he pledges that he will uphold it by attendance, prayers, gifts, and service. The minister then welcomes the new member to all the rights and privileges of church membership.

Baptism of Children and Youth

Our church provides a separate order for the baptism of children and youth, since often there are children ready to join the Church who have not been baptized in infancy. This service, while not as mature as is the office of adult baptism, does recognize that years of discretion have been reached. Children, therefore, who are baptized by this office respond for themselves when asked to take the vows.

Quite often it is necessary to baptize persons who are ill— perhaps in their homes or at a hospital. Good ministers know how to modify the service for such occasions, and extempore prayer may be a feature. The climax, of course, is the actual administration of baptism to the recumbent individual.

CHAPTER EIGHT

The Church at Work

METHODISM is faith at work. All that has been explained in the previous pages of this book—doctrine, discipline, organization—is intended to come to fruition in the activity and zeal of an energetic Christian people who seek to have God's kingdom come on earth. We are expected to make all our time—even the hours of rest and recreation—count for God. "Never be unemployed; never be triflingly employed," was John Wesley's injunction to his preachers.

In keeping with this spirit Methodism has been a stirring activist movement marked by vigor and energy both in the local congregation and in the general church. Few realize how far-reaching are its manifold activities and how sweeping its ideal. From the smallest congregation to the farthest reaches of the world parish of Methodism, the energies and personal talents of each individual are expected to find expression in doing the work of God.

There are two ways in which the church's work may be catalogued and described. One is to take it from the standpoint of the general church and classify all activity according to the major functions of church work, as missions, education, publishing interests, evangelism, and so on. Something could profitably be said about these great causes, and a brief description given of the general boards and agencies which look after them. But the other viewpoint, which shall be taken here, is to view the organizational work of the church from the standpoint of the individual member. What are the activities of his local church? How do these become part of the great structural organization of Methodism? Most important, how shall one in his local church fit into the grand purpose of God and make his life count in the congregation and community where he lives? These are supremely important questions.

One thing is certain: All the energy and zeal which infuse and sustain the larger work of the church depend on the individual church member. From where he sits in his pew on Sunday morning, though he may not know it, the long, strong lines of Methodist connectionalism are going out to encircle the world. They go to a Methodist chaplain ministering to American troops on foreign soil, to a deaconess working in a Wesley House on the Gulf Coast, to a student assisted by the Student Loan and Scholarship Fund of the Board of Education, to an editor of church-school publications planning far ahead for study material, to a lay leader busily supervising his Methodist Men. To all these and to scores of others, unknown to the ordinary church member, there radiates his influence, his help. If anyone thinks he can go to church to "get away from it all," he will soon find—happily enough both for himself and for the whole connection—that he has really gotten into it all. Even in the peace of Sunday worship one can feel the pulse-beat of the Church universal, a Church that is neither resting nor asleep, but is everywhere a living, breathing organism.

> All one body we
> One in hope and doctrine,
> One in charity.

John Wesley once said that the "Bible knows nothing of solitary religion."

The activities of the Quarterly Conference and of the Official Board have already been described. The four primary commissions which each church should have—Membership and Evangelism, Education, Missions, and Finance—have also been outlined. There are, however, other local church agencies of great importance. First and foremost is the CHURCH SCHOOL.

The Church School

Commonly called the "Sunday school," [1] this is the mightiest of all church agencies. In truth it can scarcely be called an agency at all, since it is the church itself acting as teacher of its own. The home has a teaching function, and so has the school, and so has the pulpit; but the fact remains that the Sunday-morning church school provides the only systematic, purposeful instruction in gospel truth and its application to life that Christian people usually receive.

This statement does not discount the duty of parents to inculcate in their children by precept and example the primary and fundamental lessons of Christian living; it is not to forget that every preacher is duty bound to give to both old and young systematic sermonic indoctrination; it is simply to say that the average child of the average Methodist home must be taught in the church school—if he is systematically taught at all—the deep verities of the Christian faith and of their bearing on life.

Unfortunately even the best of parents scarcely have anything like a regular plan by which they train their children to live Christianly. Usually they try to inculcate the important lessons of life, especially deep moral principles and immediate Christian duties, as each special issue arises. But

[1] Church school is the proper name for the inclusive teaching functions of all departments of each local church. Sunday school is that part of it which meets Sunday morning.

there is need for a well-integrated study of Bible truth, for the understanding of ethical problems, and for a knowledge of church-wide activities which Christian parents scarcely have time or training to give.

The public school is sometimes depended upon to train children in civic morality and ethical living. It should indeed do its part, but while at best it may be expected to teach lessons of good citizenship and the necessary virtues of honesty and fair dealing, it is handicapped even in this regard by the decision of the courts that no religion at all may be taught within its confines. This cuts the nerve of anything positive the school may do, for *without religion all ethical systems sooner or later collapse*. Only the church, basing her teaching on the everlasting gospel, can establish a proper regard for man because it teaches first one's primary obligation to God. *Unless children are taught Christian truth in the church school, they will not be taught it regularly and systematically anywhere.*

Methodism to date has not failed to realize this truth. Its Sunday schools were a part of its program from the earliest days. Susannah Wesley taught a little class of children in the Epworth rectory—including her own numerous brood— long before Robert Raikes began his first formal Sunday school. John Wesley saw to it that in his Savannah parish there was a Sunday school with regular classes.

As, later on, The Methodist Church grew, its church schools kept pace with its growth. The measure of any local church's life and vigor can best be found, not in the number of adult members on its rolls nor in the salary paid the minister, but in the number enrolled in the church school. "No matter how important a church appears to be," one of our bishops said, "if it has not got a good Sunday school, that church is on the way to the cemetery." He added, "It may take a long time to get there—but it will."

To promote and supervise Methodist church schools, the General Conference has established the Division of the Local Church of the Board of Education, and in each local church a Commission on Education. The church also provides for the publication of a complete body of church-school literature. This is systematized and graded to fit the various ages and is arranged to cover all subjects on which Christian people should be taught and informed.

In providing literature, The Methodist Church through the Editorial Division of the Board of Education co-operates with other Christian denominations in producing the International Sunday School Lessons. So general is the use of these co-ordinated lessons in Protestantism that a Methodist authority once called the church school the "greatest theological seminary in Christendom."

A successful church school depends on:

1. *The self-sacrifice and ability of officers and teachers* in each church school. Such officers and teachers must freely give their own time and attention to the work, and at considerable cost to themselves. Their Sunday, their day of rest, must be drawn upon for the sake of others. But let this be said to our church-school teachers: *The rewards are greater than the cost.* A faithful church-school teacher fulfills a mission scarcely inferior to that of the ministry itself. Many stalwart Christians today can testify to the abiding influence of some well-remembered church-school teacher during their formative years.

2. *The interest and support of the pastor and of the Official Board of the church.* Nominal interest and benevolent well-wishing are not enough. The pastor must give his time, the

officials of their means, to provide the proper facilities. It is a sad comment on any church when in connection with an imposing sanctuary the church-school rooms are comparatively bare and poorly appointed.

3. *The general attendance of the people*—old as well as young. There are classes for every age and study materials to suit all manner of needs. Methodist parents should *take* their children—not send them.

The church school is not only the training ground but the recruiting agency of the church. Out of its classes come the boys and girls who are to become church members when they reach the age of discretion; in its leadership are found the most substantial "pillars"—to use Paul's word—of any congregation. The church of the future is the church school of the present.

The Woman's Society of Christian Service

In every local church there is, or should be, a WOMAN'S SOCIETY OF CHRISTIAN SERVICE.

Practically all the organizational work of the women members of The Methodist Church is carried on through this society. This vast organization has been called the "largest women's club in the world"—and it may with some truth claim this title. In the breadth of its activities, the sweeping nature of its program, the amount of Christian work it accomplishes, and the tremendous enrollment it possesses there is nothing comparable to the "W.S.C.S." Perhaps in no other organization have women banded themselves together so efficiently as they have in the voluntary work of Methodism's Woman's Society.

Organically the Woman's Division of Christian Service— the national body to which the Woman's Societies are auxiliary—is a division of the Board of Missions. It has its own constitution, however, its own officers, its own budget (a huge one), and both in the United States and elsewhere functions as an autonomous organization. It owns and supervises schools, colleges, hospitals, homes, social centers, orphanages, rescue homes, and mission stations in many "faraway places with strange-sounding names." It has its own corps of missionaries and deaconesses who, after being commissioned under the authority of the general church, are supported and directed by the Woman's Division.

In each local church the Woman's Society provides for Methodist women their most natural channel for religious activity. It is not true to say that the Woman's Society affords the *only* sphere of activity for Methodist women. Women serve as stewards, trustees, Sunday-school superintendents and teachers, and frequently represent the church in Annual and General Conferences, and on the committees and commissions of the general church. It is a fact, however, that the W.S.C.S. in its varied program and comprehensive interests, provides each woman of the church with an opportunity to use her personal talents to best advantage.

The purpose of the Woman's Society of Christian Service, as stated in the *Discipline,* is:

To develop and maintain Christian work among women and children at home and abroad.

To cultivate Christian family life.

To enlist and organize the efforts of Christian women, youth, and children in behalf of native and foreign groups, needy childhood, and community welfare.

To assist in the promotion of a missionary spirit throughout the church.

To select, train, and maintain Christian workers.

To co-operate with the local church in its responsibilities.

To seek fellowship with Christian women of this and other lands in establishing a Christian social order around the world.

In keeping with this announced aim the society in the local church divides its work and responsibilities into various departments. These are: promotion, missionary education, Christian social relations, local-church activities, student work, youth work, children's work, spiritual life, literature and publications, and supply work. In charge of each of these functions of its program the local-church society yearly elects a "secretary," who is the executive of that particular department and who usually has a committee of other women to help her (for example, the "secretary of spiritual life," the "secretary of promotion").

Of course the local society elects its president, vice-presidents, recording secretary, and treasurers. Meetings are held regularly, and the general educational and promotional program of the society is systematically put into effect. The mission-study classes of the Woman's Society of Christian Service, with their regular and comprehensive coverage year by year of special fields of work, have been of untold value in deepening and broadening the mind of the whole church.

Women of the church who are gainfully employed and so cannot attend day meetings are organized into the Wesleyan Service Guild. This gives them an opportunity to participate in a program of work and in leadership which otherwise would not be open to them. The Wesleyan Service Guild is a distinctive part of the women's organization.

The Woman's Society of Christian Service through the systematic giving of its members and the careful management and expenditure of its funds is able to carry on a colossal program. The amount contributed for foreign- and home-mission work in any one year runs into several millions, and twice as much is contributed by the women to their own local churches.[2] The average official board member, when told what the Woman's Society of Christian Service in his own church gives to all causes in any one year, is apt to express both admiration and amazement.

It is the goal of the Woman's Society of Christian Service to enlist every Methodist woman in its ranks. The Woman's Society of Christian Service has been growing in numbers each year. At last reporting[3] there were 1,786,566 members and a budget of $7,763,487.49.

Lay Activities

The Methodist Church is a layman's church. While ministers in the last reported statistics numbered 26,165, the lay membership of the church was 9,223,152. Laymen have equal representation with the ministers in the great General and Jurisdictional Conferences, and thus share equal responsibility in making laws, electing church executives, and shaping general policies. In Quarterly and District Conferences and, of course, in the Official Board, laymen comprise the great majority of the members and do their full part in all matters coming before these respective bodies.

"Lay activities," Bishop Costen J. Harrell properly states, "is a program rather than a society." And what a program! The General Board of Lay Activities, having charge over laymen's work, puts into effect in each local church a comprehensive and far-reaching plan. In the *Discipline* this is outlined as follows:

1. Christian stewardship

[2] In 1950 the W.S.C.S. gave to the Woman's Division of the General Board $6,522,278 and to their local churches $13,503,292. In 1951 it gave $7,168,072 to the Woman's Division and $14,191,878 locally. In 1952 it gave $7,943,455 and $15,205,108; in 1953, $8,316,335 and $16,168,693.

[3] May 31, 1954.

2. Christian fellowship
3. Personal evangelism
4. Lay speaking or preaching
5. The circulation of church papers and other Christian literature
6. The benevolences (meaning the general financial support of the church)
7. Adequate support of the ministry
8. Sound church finance in the local church
9. Attendance upon worship services
10. Men's work
11. The training of official boards
12. The Christianizing of personal and community life
13. Co-operation with other general boards and agencies
14. District and conference lay organizations to make more effective the entire program of lay activities

It is sometimes assumed that if a man is not a steward or a trustee, he will not find the opportunity to do systematic, constructive work for his church. This is not true. To utilize the vast man-power of Methodism, the General Conference created a men's organization known as METHODIST MEN and at the same time outlined for it a broad program of lay activities.

It is the responsibility of the Official Board in each church in co-operation with the pastor and lay leader to organize a chapter of Methodist Men. The special responsibility of Methodist Men is to promote stewardship, personal evangelism, and lay speaking. Especially committed to its care is the stewardship-of-possessions program, which emphasizes the need and worth of tithing in Christian giving.

The chairman of Methodist Men is an ex-officio steward

in every church. At last reporting there were 7,300 chapters of Methodist Men with 335,000 members.

The church lay leader. Every church has a LAY LEADER, who is elected yearly by the Official Board. The lay leader has no organization as such over which he presides but is an independent officer of the church. He is thus able to promote, in co-operation with the pastor and board chairman, the entire program of lay activities.

The lay leader may be elected chairman of the Official Board, or as is more commonly the case, the chairman of the board is automatically made lay leader. This of course cannot be done where the pastor is chairman of the board.

The lay leader in a circuit charge is elected by the Quarterly Conference; the district lay leader, by the Annual Conference on nomination of the district superintendents and conference lay leader. The Annual Conference lay leader is elected by the conference on nomination of the Conference Board of Lay Activities. In each jurisdiction there is a jurisdictional secretary of lay activities, and in the general church there is an executive secretary of the Board of Lay Activities for the whole connection.

Interest in laymen's work apart from Official Board duties has grown in The Methodist Church during recent years. It may be expected to increase even more as the church continues to enlarge its program.

Methodist Finances and General Funds

"The work of the church requires the support of our people, and participation therein through service and gifts is a Christian duty and a means of grace." So the book of *Discipline* introduces its important directions regarding the financial system of The Methodist Church. In that system there are:

GENERAL FUNDS—Determined by the General Conference and raised by the whole Church to carry on its connectional work (missions, education, and so on).

ANNUAL CONFERENCE FUNDS—Determined by each Annual Conference and used to carry on special Annual Conference causes (orphanage, conference paper, and so on).

LOCAL CHURCH FUNDS—Determined by the Official Board and/or the Quarterly Conference to carry on the work of the local church (minister's salary, janitor, fuel, church repair, and so on).

In addition there may be *jurisdictional funds*, if a Jurisdictional Conference decides to ask its component Annual Conferences and charges to support some special jurisdictional project (as a headquarter's office or executive secretary). Or there may be *district funds*, from which district stewards may make apportionments for the district superintendent or for a district parsonage or for carrying on district missionary work.

Since all funds and budgets are eventually to be raised by the members of the local churches, it is the practice of many churches to incorporate in the local-church budget the total amount that the church is expected to give to all causes. Thus the dollar in the collection plate is subject to division and subdivision until a proportionate part of it has been put into every approved activity of the general and local church.

THE GENERAL FUNDS

The big general funds and budgets of The Methodist Church are four in number. They must each be prepared and recommended to the General Conference by the Council on World Service and Finance. When adopted by the General

Conference, they become the general budget of the church for the ensuing four years.

The General Conference also decides the basis on which each fund is to be apportioned to the Annual Conferences or to the local church. Most funds are based upon a fixed budget—that is, one which has been estimated and adopted in advance as an over-all amount to be raised during the year or perhaps during the next four years. Most of the general boards of the church, however, receive a set percentage of the World Service dollar as World Service funds come in. These percentages are fixed by each General Conference for the ensuing four years and must be strictly adhered to. They can be deviated from only in direst emergency.

Succeeding General Conferences revise the general church budget and vary the respective percentages each board or agency gets as need may demand. New causes and new funds may of course be provided for by future General Conferences as new situations arise.

At present the four established general funds are:

The World Service Fund—This gigantic fund [4] supports all the World Service agencies of the church. These agencies are such organizations as the Board of Missions, Board of Education, theological schools, Board of Pensions, and so on.

The General Administration Fund—This provides for the expenses of the General Conference sessions, the Judicial Council, the statistical office, and such commissions and committees as may be constituted by the General Conference. This enables them to do their work through the four years until the next General Conference meets.

The Episcopal Fund—This fund supports the bishops, re-

[4] The total budget of the World Service Fund for the 1952-56 quadrennium is $9,660,000 per year.

tired bishops, widows of bishops, and minor children of deceased bishops. It is obtained by the General Conference asking from each Annual Conference an amount equal to a fixed percentage—at present 2 per cent—of the total of the salaries paid the ministers of that conference. The Annual Conferences may apportion out this amount to the local churches on any basis they please, but usually they follow the percentage-against-the-minister's-salary plan just as the General Conference has handed it down to them.

The Interdenominational Co-operation Fund—This is the church's contribution to the work of the National Council of Churches and the World Council of Churches.

ANNUAL CONFERENCE FUNDS

As has been explained, each Annual Conference has the right to establish its own budget for Annual Conference benevolences and causes. This budget is drawn up and presented by the Annual Conference Commission on World Service and Finance after that commission has inquired into all the causes which the conference may be expected to support. When approved and adopted, this becomes the Annual Conference Benevolence Budget. Its funds are used chiefly for projects within the conference, and there is no overlapping between the items of the Annual Conference Benevolence Budget and that of the general funds.

However, in assigning to each local church its share of the general and conference benevolence budget, it is mandatory to put these two funds together and apportion out the combined amount as the World Service and Conference Benevolence budget. Here is how this is done: Each local church is notified at the beginning of each conference year what amount has been apportioned to it for its share of the combined budget. The *Discipline* suggests that the pastor and lay leader shall thereupon "present" to the church—and to every church on a circuit—the amount asked, with an explanation of each cause to be supported. So ample opportunity is given for a discussion of the local-church apportionment *before* it is officially put before the Quarterly Conference. The members of that conference are therefore ready, when the apportionments are presented, to accept, to increase, or to lower the amount their charge is asked to assume.

In practice, since the element of compulsion is not present and since the apportionments are made by conference and district representatives who know what is equitable, charges usually take pride in assuming the amount expected of them. Often stewards assume more than is asked. Even more often, churches overpay at year's end their apportionments.

Methodists are encouraged to give to special causes or special interests when these are properly approved by the General Church or Annual Conference Commission on World Service and Finance. An amount paid to a "special"—say for a mission building in Cuba or for the salary of a medical missionary in Malaya—can be credited to the local church's share of general funds if properly authorized and sent through the proper channels. Special appeals for causes not listed in the regular budgets of the church are looked upon with disfavor except in cases of emergency. Indeed, the *Discipline* directs that no appeal can be made to a local church unless the cause represented has been properly approved by the Budget Commission. Since all worthy causes are expected to be reviewed by the commissions formulating the budget, it is assumed that the causes which the respective budget commissions approve are in every way worthy, and that causes which have not been approved should not be allowed to make special appeals to local churches. This blocks out sporadic pleas and casual collections taken publicly in church, and enables Methodists to underwrite and support in a stronger way those Christian moves and projects of the most value.

It is evident from the above that when a Methodist puts his dollar in the collection plate as part of his pledge for the year, it is divided into many parts. Usually the greater part of it goes to the local church. Of the rest the District and the Annual Conference, and always the big funds of the world-wide Church, each get a certain share. "We give," states the *Discipline*, "that all members of The Methodist Church may share in its manifold ministries at home and abroad, and that the work committed to us may prosper."

World Service Agencies

The agencies of the Church which are known as world service agencies because supported by the World Service Fund are the BOARD OF MISSIONS (largest of all the boards), BOARD OF EDUCATION, BOARD OF EVANGELISM, BOARD OF LAY ACTIVITIES, BOARD OF TEMPERANCE, BOARD OF WORLD PEACE, BOARD OF HOSPITALS AND HOMES, BOARD OF SOCIAL AND ECONOMIC RELATIONS, BOARD OF PENSIONS, RADIO AND FILM COMMISSION, AMERICAN BIBLE SOCIETY (with other denominations).

Each receives a proportionate part of the World Service Fund receipts according to a percentage scale adopted by the General Conference. The COUNCIL ON WORLD SERVICE AND FINANCE acts as a sort of budget commission for the whole Church.

It is not within the scope of this book to give a detailed study of the organization, structure, and work of these boards or of other important agencies. Reference must be made to the *Discipline* for full information on these and other important features of the Church's life.

CHAPTER NINE

Methodists and Other Churches

METHODISTS enjoy co-operating with other Christian churches. We have been foremost in moves looking toward Christian unity. The Ecumenical movement—the trend toward union of all Protestant churches—is being supported in every way by Methodists. While we hold tenaciously to our beliefs, we grant all other Christians the right to hold to theirs provided that they show by deed and profession that they are sincere followers of Jesus Christ. We, therefore, respect one another's Christian fellowship, covet one another's good will, appreciate the opportunity to join in others' worship and have them join us in ours.

We put up no bars preventing members of another church from partaking of the sacrament with us, but are glad to have them. We extend the right hand of fellowship to all sincere seekers, but we do not proselytize those who belong to another Christian communion. When members of other Christian churches profess a desire to join ours we receive such persons without requiring them to renew any of the Christian vows they had taken when first they joined their church. When one of our own members wishes to unite with another church, we give him a letter commending him to the love and care of the church which he wishes to join. "Break not the brotherhood" is a Methodist principle.

The Methodist Church has an official Commission on

Church Union, with full power "to consider specific overtures or proposals for organic union with other denominations, . . . to initiate studies looking toward organic union, to confer with representatives of other denominations in any general discussion of church union, to encourage interdenominational co-operation throughout the church." Our church contributes financially to such common causes as the American Bible Society, the World Council of Churches, and the National Council of Churches. The first president of the Federal Council of Churches, organized in 1908, was a Methodist bishop, Eugene R. Hendrix. Since that time Methodist officials and representatives have been leaders in all the work of the Federal Council, the World Council, and now the National Council of Churches.

Since our people live among and wish to cultivate and continue friendly relations with all religious groups, it will be helpful to set forth in the following pages our attitude toward the doctrines and practices of other large churches. It is obviously impossible to treat here all the churches and sects met with in American life. The following five churches have been taken because of their numbers and influence, and their close social and economic contacts with our people.

Methodists and Roman Catholics

We believe the Roman Catholic Church to be a true church of Jesus Christ, but that it is weighted down and covered over with practices and doctrines representing much more the tradition of men than the truth of God. We respect and admire that church for some of its tenets and practices, but we differ profoundly from it in others.

We are one with Roman Catholics in allegiance to God as Father, to Christ as Lord and Saviour, and to the Holy Spirit as guide and counselor. We believe in a holy catholic Church, but that Church is to us broad and universal, never narrow nor exclusive. We join with the Roman Catholics in reverencing saintly men and women of the past who set an example to all of us; we appreciate the unremitting missionary efforts of Roman Catholicism and its vast works of charity carried on in hospitals, orphanages, rescue homes, and the like. We admire the peculiar type of personal piety which Rome often cultivates among its people and the deep saintliness frequently manifest. Above all, we appreciate the way in which the Roman Catholic Church holds up the cross of Christ and exalts the sacrifice of our Lord at all times and in all places.

We are indebted to it for former leadership in the field of scholarship and for keeping the lamp of learning bright through the Dark Ages; for its ancient cathedrals which to the historically minded represent an undivided Christendom; for its insistence on strict morality, on the sanctity of marriage, on moves for moral and social betterment led by such groups as the Holy Name Society and the Legion of Decency.

But we *differ completely* with the Roman Catholics:

1. In their dependence on an earthly church and on the bishop of Rome as the final authority in matters of religion. We deprecate the doctrine that the pope is infallible when he speaks *ex cathedra*, that is, formally and officially, since he is merely a man. We deplore the dominance of the priesthood in the Roman Church and its teaching that a priest has power to grant absolution for sins. We hold that every man is his own priest and that all believers constitute a priesthood whose influence and leadership help each to live closer to God.

2. We deny the Roman Catholic teaching that Christ's body is made to appear in the Mass at the word of the priest; we consider it a ridiculous travesty to worship relics or bless

medals or use "holy water." We deplore the idea that man can be saved by what he does and are afraid that the entire Roman Catholic system becomes in effect a salvation-by-works process.

3. We deny that one can be truly pardoned from sin by doing penance or may gain merit by performing pilgrimages or lighting candles or making vows; we deny that there is a purgatory and consider it wrong to say masses for the dead.

4. We object fiercely to the assumption by Rome that it alone is the Church and that only its bishops and priests are true ministers of God. We deny that Rome can even claim to be catholic, for catholicity is *in*clusive and not *ex*clusive, as the Roman Church makes it.

5. We object to the Roman Catholic practice of forbidding people to hear opposing points of view or to read books which set forth what they consider hostile doctrine. Especially do we object to the Roman plan of silencing by persecution or menace the preaching and teaching of other faiths in those lands where they have control. We hold to the American principles of the open Bible, the open forum, the unfettered press, and the unhindered spread of ideas. We believe that truth is its own best witness and that Christian people should be allowed to sift for themselves all ideas affecting their own welfare. History makes clear that the countries which have long been under Roman Catholic domination have failed to grow intellectually, morally, and even physically. Complete Roman Catholic dominance, we cannot avoid feeling, is a blight on Christian liberty and a pall on human progress.

6. We discourage marriage between Protestants and Roman Catholics, feeling that such marriages, while sometimes successful, always are threatened with heartache and family dissension. The Roman Catholic party to a mixed marriage is

under the dominance of the priest and either must obey his instructions with regard to bringing up children and in all the intimate matters of the home, or must refuse to obey them. In either case there is unhappiness and tension. "Don't marry a Roman Catholic" is a sound injunction for Methodist youth to keep in mind.

It is clear, therefore, that we are in disagreement with many Roman Catholic beliefs, but that by no means implies a personal hostility toward Roman Catholics as individuals. They are our friends and neighbors, and we shall trust them as such. We are at variance with their *system*, not with *them*.

Methodists and Episcopalians

Methodists are closely akin to Episcopalians doctrinally and liturgically, as both Churches originated in the Church of England and inherited the same rites and the same Articles of Religion. That there are great psychological differences between the two is undeniable, but these great Churches have learned more and more to appreciate each other.

Methodists admire the Protestant Episcopal Church:

1. For its emphasis on the Church as the Body of Christ. Representing an entity which transcends and holds together all local churches in one august body is the Church—Holy, Catholic, and Universal—not a congeries of separate, local congregations, but a transcendent unity, the Bride of Christ.

2. For its *Book of Common Prayer* and a stately ritual in which words and ideas are fittingly blended in a majestic offering of praise and worship.

3. For the way in which by systematic and well-chosen readings and lessons from the Holy Bible the people are guided through the church year. Each season has its own special mes-

sage, each emphasizes some part of the work of Christ for his Church.

4. For the wise use of symbol in building and altar, the reverence for the house of God, giving to God, through worship, of our very best—in all these things we deeply appreciate the contribution of the Protestant Episcopal Church to the Church universal.

We disagree with the Protestant Episcopal Church over:

1. The doctrine of apostolic succession. This doctrine holds that from the days of the apostles on there has been a chain of ordinations with one generation of bishops ordaining another and these in turn ordaining priests, so that the Church's orders go back in uninterrupted succession to the time of the apostles. This theory, John Wesley once said, "No one ever has proved, nor can prove."

2. We disagree with the belief that no one can administer the sacrament nor can be truly ordained except by one who is in the apostolic succession. We affirm that God only knows whom he has truly ordained and that the "test of apostolic succession is apostolic success."

3. We do not favor too much rigidity in worship even when a stately prayer book furnishes the norm. We adopt robes and vestments and a clerical dress for certain functional purposes, but Methodists are still afraid of "formality."

4. We do not follow the Protestant Episcopal idea that the office of bishop is a "third Order," thus making the bishop an ecclesiastical superior to his brethren. In Methodism the bishop is an elder set apart to be an administrator, having no unique spiritual power save the right to ordain—and his power to ordain must be granted in each instance by Annual Conference vote. This power is something given by the Church to the bishop, not by the bishop to the Church.

5. We do not believe that in order to join the Church, one must be confirmed by the laying on of hands of a bishop, though we respect Confirmation. We receive persons into the church through our pastors, and while our Reception of Members is a close replica of the Office of Confirmation in the Protestant Episcopal Church, there are profound differences between the underlying philosophies manifest in these separate rites.

Nevertheless Methodists and Episcopalians feel a close kinship which the years have served to deepen. Each has influenced the other to the advantage of both.

Methodists and Baptists

Methodists and Baptists are at one in their common evangelical heritage and purpose; in their deep conviction regarding the fatherhood of God, the lordship of Christ, the presence of the Holy Spirit, the Bible as the Word of life, and the need to live lives which show forth the glory and promise of the gospel.

We appreciate the Baptists:

1. For their emphasis on the sacrament of baptism—though not upon the insistence in some of their churches upon immersion as the only mode. It can be truly said that as their name implies, the Baptists have built their church largely about a Sacrament of Christ.

2. For their intense loyalty to their own fellowship. Baptists have no "connection," as we Methodists would term it. "There is no Baptist Church," said one of their authorities. "There are only Baptist churches." Yet these churches stick together in a tight comradeship which can teach much to other denominations more highly centralized in their form of organization.

3. For their aggressive gospel proclamation, evangelistic zeal, and making religious real in national life. Where other fellowships may falter and fail in political or economic moves for civic and national righteousness, you can count on the Baptists. Methodists and Baptists traditionally have stood shoulder to shoulder in all battles for public morality.

We differ with the Baptists:

1. In the insistence in most of their churches upon immersion as the only valid mode of baptism (see page 150). We do not sympathize with the practice which certain Baptist churches (though not all) follow of "close communion"— that is, of admitting only baptized (immersed) Christians to their Communion table; and we deplore the exclusiveness which inevitably appears among those who insist that a particular rite (baptism by immersion) is the only true gateway to the Church. Any insistence on the mechanics of a rite denatures the spirit of it.

2. We do not agree with their once greatly stressed teaching —or that of certain of their theologians—that when once a person has been saved from sin, he will ever after remain saved to the end. We wish that this might prove true, but experience and life teach otherwise. In the Baptist view a believer who later falls has never been saved at all. Obviously there is no way to tell whether he has or has not, but to a Methodist this theory does not comport with reason or with life.

3. We differ, or have differed, with the Baptists when they call in question the Methodist teaching that we are expected to live sinless lives. Certain Baptist leaders and theologians have held that the commandments of God are given as guides and ideals, but that it is not expected that these commandments can be kept. Against this challenge to the doctrine of

perfection our Methodist fathers heatedly responded by saying that God would not have given us commands he did not expect us to obey.

In spite of these differences Methodists and Baptists socially and economically are much the same sort of people. They have worked together well and will continue to work together in all moves for social and national betterment and for bringing on earth the kingdom of God.

Methodists and Presbyterians

With Presbyterians we traditionally have differed in doctrine, but worked well together in practice. The doctrinal differences have lain chiefly in the heavy Calvinistic emphasis insisted on by Presbyterians of an earlier day. Then an iron-clad predestination was opposed to Methodism's affirmation of universal atonement. As the years have gone by and the Calvinistic emphasis has been softened, Methodist and Presbyterian congregations have drawn much closer together. In patterns of worship, in social, political, and economic issues, we are perhaps closer to the Presbyterians than to any other large body of Christians.

Methodists appreciate:

1. The Presbyterians' emphasis on the sovereignty of God, so long as that sovereignty is not thought of as destroying the freedom of man's will. Over against the weak teaching of certain modern liberals that God is unable to break through his own natural laws, or that he is the embodiment of a supine benevolence, the Presbyterians rightly see God high and lifted up, the sovereign Ruler and majestic Creator of the universe. The Church universal needs to have that truth stressed.

2. The solid racial stock behind the Presbyterians—Dutch, Swiss, and especially Scottish—the sturdy way their ancestors

fought both against the papal power and in Scotland against the Church of England when their Christian liberty was imperiled. There has always been considerable iron in the Presbyterian blood, and Christianity is richer for it.

3. Their emphasis on learning and on an educated ministry. They have put into practice John Wesley's celebrated exhortation "Let us unite the two so long divided—knowledge and vital piety." Presbyterians have always demanded that their ministers be well-trained men, and the universities in Scotland and the famous institutions they have built in our own land witness to the intensity of their search for truth. We can thank their scholars for leadership in many fields of Christian interest.

Methodists disagree with the Presbyterians whenever they so emphasize the sovereignty of God as to permit logic to supplant fact in viewing Christian experience. Also we do not like a certain rigidity that is sometimes found in Presbyterian thought, nor the regimentation of their theological and ministerial mind under the stamp of a fixed educated process. These features, however, are not as obtrusive today as formerly, and our people live more and more in Christian unity with the Presbyterians.

Methodists and Lutherans

The Lutheran Church is largely composed of those whose forebears came from Germany or the Scandinavian countries. Lutheran congregations have never become as widely distributed over the United States as have some of the other Protestant denominations. Nevertheless Lutherans are unusually strong in certain localities, especially where immigration brought large numbers from Germany or Northern Europe.

Methodists and Lutherans agree on all the important verities of Christianity as these are stated in the Apostles' Creed. Especially do we appreciate the Lutherans for the seriousness of their pastoral leadership. It means something to a Lutheran home for the pastor to make a call, and there is nothing perfunctory about his visit. He may examine the children as to their Christian attitudes, or he may enjoin the parents as to some special duty they should perform. He takes seriously his duty as pastor, and so do the people.

Lutherans guard well the table of the Lord, and while they admit others than Lutherans to their sacramental services, they let it be known that this is no light privilege.

Lutherans because of their training and their racial heritage do not easily become members of other Protestant churches. Their indoctrination and organization tend to build them into a more self-centered communion than characterizes the usual American church. Nevertheless they are a solid Christian people whose personal piety, training, and character we may well emulate.

Methodists and Smaller Church Bodies

Sufficient has already been written concerning Methodist doctrine and polity to make clear what attitude Methodists may be expected to take toward church bodies not treated in the pages above. In matters of polity (internal church organization) we all agree that each church has a right to decide for itself what form of government it shall have. There is therefore no quarrel with any body of Christians who may prefer a congregational polity (in which the congregation by democratic rule manages everything) or presbyterial (in which a group of elders direct matters) or episcopal (with bishops as chief officers). Curiously enough, Methodist polity is a combination of these three organizational forms. We would never claim, however, that our polity is better than that of others. We simply say that it suits us best, and we will respect the claim of any other Christian group which says the same for its organizational pattern.

Methodists have frequent contact with certain of the so-called enthusiastic sects and with minor groups which emphasize what they believe to be New Testament manifestations of spiritual phenomena appearing among them. Some of these bodies stemmed out of the Methodist movement in years past. It behooves us to deal gently with them. We appreciate the zeal, the intensity, and the announced quest for holiness among those groups which make this last their aim and ideal. We deprecate a certain narrowness and exclusiveness shown by many of these smaller bodies and feel that their crass literalism precludes them from taking advantage of the broadness and sweep of a true catholic, or universal, Christianity. They do much good work, however, and shame us by going into situations and among people whom Methodism does not seem to reach as it once did.

The Methodist Church and World-Wide Methodism

Methodism has spread over the world and is at home in almost every land. Separate Methodist churches have of course been organized. Some of these are very large bodies. While holding to the same doctrine and rules of personal discipline, these churches differ from one another markedly in forms of organization. British Methodism, for instance, has no bishops; and neither had the Canadian Methodists before they went into the Church of Canada.

The Methodist churches of the world send representatives periodically to a World Methodist Conference, which meets once every five years. This conference, while having no power to pass any laws that may be binding upon its constituent members, gives an opportunity for fellowship and fraternity, and for considering all that affects present-day Methodism everywhere. Its endeavor is to deepen mutual understanding and to encourage and inspire the world-wide brotherhood of the followers of Wesley.

The World Methodist Conference elects a World Methodist Council, which is empowered to prepare and plan for succeeding World Methodist Conferences. The council also acts as an advisory group dealing with all questions that may arise among Methodist bodies in different nations. Within recent years world Methodism has become much better integrated than ever before through its world conferences and its World Methodist Council. Wesley's dream of a world parish is becoming a reality to the Methodists who continue to carry on his work—and God's—in our day.

Goals for a Christian's Striving

To *know* God and settle my soul's salvation once and for all with a deep, quiet, assured trust that nothing can take away. This above all—this above all!

To *live* so that all my time may count for God and his Plan for my life—in business or pleasure, asleep or awake, in youth or age, in great things or small, to do the Father's will and in that will find my peace.

To *keep* alive the spiritual glow of true Christianity by prayer and devotions, Bible reading, grace at meals, systematic and unfailing attendance at church, fulfilling daily all spiritual duties.

To *advance* God's kingdom, beginning in my own life but moving at once to think and live for others in family, community, and nation—to right wrong, help the helpless, bind up the brokenhearted, give generously, love the brotherhood.

To *learn* through home and church and school and books and life's own experiences a richer wisdom as time goes by—that mind and soul, according well, may abound more and more in all knowledge and understanding, even to the understanding of the deep things of both man and God.

To *leave* to God the things I cannot know nor am meant to know, in sure and certain trust that he who created this world and called us into being, even the God and Father of our Lord Jesus Christ, will keep and perfect in his own time them that are his—in life, in death, in that vast forever. Even so, Father, keep thou us all.

Index